I0796866

Hillary Phillips dropped a gem with *My Brain While Reading the Bible*. This is definitely not your typical Bible study! It's real talk, laugh-out-loud funny, and straight-up honest. She flips the script, making ancient Bible characters feel like present-day people. Her storytelling makes the Word pop off the page, and her vivid reflections hit different—fresh like new music! If you're ready to own your imperfections, find grace for your journey, and vibe deeper with God, this book should be your next read! Do not sleep on it!

Rickey "Slikk Muzik" Offord, four-time Grammy Award–winning music producer

I've had the pleasure of working with Hillary for many years, and I can truly say this about her: she is 100 percent authentic in her love for God and her joy in sharing his Word. This book is further proof of that fact, and I'm sure you'll enjoy it as much as I did!

Butch Hartman, creator of *The Fairly OddParents*, *Danny Phantom*, *The Garden Cartoon*, and more

Hillary's voice is refreshing, witty, and Spirit-led. *My Brain While Reading the Bible* invites you to engage with Scripture with honesty and humor, making God's Word feel personal, powerful, and beautifully relevant.

Jacqueline Horbrook, M.Ed., founder and CEO of Black Christian Influencers, Inc.

What I love about *My Brain While Reading the Bible* is how Hillary breaks down the living Word in a way that's both true and simplified. She makes Scripture feel real and relatable, bringing it straight into everyday life! Hillary is hilarious in real life, and her same humor and heart come through in the book.

Whitney Moss, Christian influencer and CEO of Pretty Belle Enterprises, LLC

Hillary brings fun yet refreshing hot takes to Scripture that will make you laugh, think deeper, and love God's Word that much more. Such a fun read!

Hailey Julia, speaker, entertainer, entrepreneur, and founder of My Bible Buddies

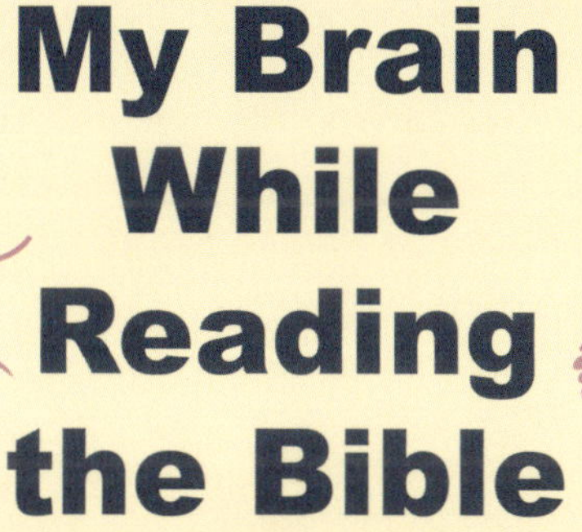

My Brain While Reading the Bible

Hot Takes on My Favorite Scriptures

Hillary Phillips

A 40-DAY DEVOTIONAL

BroadStreet
PUBLISHING

BroadStreet Publishing® Group, LLC
Savage, Minnesota, USA
BroadStreetPublishing.com

My Brain While Reading the Bible: Hot Takes on My Favorite Scriptures
Copyright © 2025 Hillary Caitlyn Phillips

9781424569595 (faux leather)
9781424569601 (ebook)

All rights reserved. No part of this publication may be reproduced, distributed, or transmitted in any form or by any means, including photocopying, recording, or other electronic or mechanical methods, without the prior written permission of the publisher, except in the case of brief quotations embodied in critical reviews and certain other noncommercial uses permitted by copyright law. No portion of this book may be used or reproduced in any way for the purpose of training artificial intelligence technologies. As per Article 4(3) of the Digital Single Market Directive 2019/790, BroadStreet Publishing reserves this work from the text and data mining exception.

Scripture quotations marked NKJV are taken from the New King James Version®. Copyright © 1982 by Thomas Nelson. Used by permission. All rights reserved. Scripture quotations marked NLT are taken from the Holy Bible, New Living Translation. Copyright © 1996, 2004, 2015 by Tyndale House Foundation. Used by permission of Tyndale House Publishers, a Division of Tyndale House Ministries, Carol Stream, Illinois 60188. All rights reserved. Scripture quotations marked NIV are taken from The Holy Bible, New International Version® NIV®. Copyright © 1973, 1978, 1984, 2011 by Biblica, Inc.™ Used by permission. All rights reserved worldwide. Scripture quotations marked ESV are taken from the ESV® Bible (The Holy Bible, English Standard Version®). Copyright © 2001 by Crossway, a publishing ministry of Good News Publishers. Used by permission. All rights reserved. Scripture quotations marked NASB are taken from the New American Standard Bible®. Copyright © 1960, 1962, 1963, 1968, 1971, 1972, 1973, 1975, 1977, 1995, 2020 by The Lockman Foundation. Used by permission. www.Lockman.org. Scripture quotations marked CSB are taken from the Christian Standard Bible®. Copyright © 2017 by Holman Bible Publishers. Used by permission. Christian Standard Bible®, and CSB® are federally registered trademarks of Holman Bible Publishers. All rights reserved.

Cover and interior by Garborg Design Works | garborgdesign.com

Printed in China

25 26 27 28 29 5 4 3 2 1

To everyone who has ever felt disconnected from God or the Bible, this book is for you. May you find yourself in these stories, and may they lead you closer to Jesus.

Contents

Introduction

Welcome to this forty-day devotional journey, a journey that's as much about exploring the Bible as it is about exploring ourselves.

The Bible is so much more than a book with epic stories. It is the living Word of God and holds the power to transform lives. It is a collection of sixty-six holy books that tell the story of God and his relationship to humankind, and it provides us with an opportunity to draw closer to him, learn what he has to say, and gain perspective on what he thinks. God is our refuge, our deliverer, our Abba Father, and our friend. His Word is our strength, and when we allow it to expose our areas of weakness, we gain a deeper understanding of our need for Jesus.

This devotional is meant to be more than just a daily reading assignment—it's an invitation to engage with the Bible in a dynamic and personal way. My hope is that it helps you recognize that the beauty of the Bible is not only found in its divine inspiration but also in its raw humanity.

It's easy to read the Word and think of biblical figures as stoic, untouchable heroes or icons of faith. But these were real people with real problems—

just like you and me. The more we understand the human experiences of biblical figures, the more we see ourselves in their stories. We can learn from their mistakes, find victory through their triumphs, become inspired by their faith, and, like them, feel comforted by God's grace.

As you embark on this devotional journey, I encourage you to read through the Bible with fresh eyes. Whether you have heard a story countless times or find yourself reading something new, invite God to open your eyes to see things you haven't seen before. I encourage you to look for the humanity in each story and take a moment to put yourself in the same shoes—or sandals.

While you read, think about what it would look like if the exact stories, God-given commands, or miraculous events were to take place in our modern-day world. Imagine how you and others would respond. If you turned on the news and learned that someone had parted the Red Sea with nothing but a staff or slew a giant with a tiny stone, how would you feel?

Picture the facial expressions and imagine the voices of the people in these stories. Envisioning this might make you chuckle, but it can also help you recognize just how relatable the events of the Bible really are. You will find that, while these ancient people didn't have the same kind of modern struggles that we have, their struggles were just as real, and they were just as human as we are. Times and culture have changed, but our need for God remains the same.

Each day's entry is designed to be relatable, thought-provoking, and sometimes even a little humorous. It is my prayer that you feel free to laugh, cry, reflect, and grow. Whether you read these devotions in order or choose to skip around, my hope is that you'll find something that speaks to you right where you are and that the Lord encounters you and ministers to your heart through Scripture.

So, I invite you to come as you are—no pretenses, no need for perfection. Bring your questions, your doubts, your joys, and your struggles. Together, let's explore these Bible stories, some of which might make us scratch our heads but teach us valuable lessons. Let's find the wisdom God has for us and see how we can apply it to our lives today.

We'll reflect on areas where we need to surrender. We'll wrestle with our own doubts and fears, and we'll celebrate the moments of faith that bring us closer to God. I'll also share personal stories that connect with biblical narratives, offering lessons that have shaped my own journey with God. And yes, we'll have some fun along the way.

By sharing what happens in my brain while reading the Bible, I hope it leads you to reflect on the thoughts that arise in your own brain while reading as well. Ultimately, I pray that God will use this devotional to fill you with a greater appreciation for his Word and a deeper understanding of his unfailing love for you.

Hillary Phillips

1

What's the Manna with You?

The Lord *said to Moses, "I will rain down bread from heaven for you. The people are to go out each day and gather enough for that day."*

Exodus 16:4 NIV

If there is one book in the Bible that might lead people to pull out their hair—or, for some of us, snatch off our wigs—it's the book of Exodus. In Exodus, God continuously demonstrates his unparalleled power but is repeatedly met with disobedience, forgetfulness, and rejection. The Israelites, freshly freed from the chains of Egypt, quickly forget the miracles that led to their escape: the ten plagues, the parting of the Red Sea, and God's provision of water while they were in the middle of the desert.

Only two months after they were miraculously freed, the Israelites continued to complain, saying, "If only we had died by the Lord's hand in Egypt! There we sat around pots of meat and ate all the food we wanted, but you have brought us out into this desert to starve this entire assembly to death" (Exodus 16:3). It's almost comical, isn't it? The Israelites were not only sassy but also entitled. These people had just witnessed the most incredible events in history, but the moment their stomachs started grumbling, their mouths did too.

In his mercy, God heard the Israelites' plea and said to Moses, "I have heard the complaints of the children of Israel. Speak to them, saying, 'At twilight you shall eat meat, and in the morning you shall be filled with bread. And you shall know that I *am* the LORD your God'" (Exodus 16:12 NKJV). And just like that, God provided. This manna was unlike anything they had ever experienced. It was a physical sign of God's care and provision. It was fresh every morning (Lamentations 3:22–23), perfectly timed and perfectly portioned to meet their daily needs.

But instead of responding with gratitude for this miraculous provision, the Israelites began to grumble again. They longed for the days back in Egypt, remembering the pots of meat and the food they once had. Had they lost their minds? These people were *slaves* in Egypt, *oppressed* and *mistreated*, yet their discomfort in the wilderness led them to do something many of us do today. They began to romanticize the place that God delivered them from.

When life gets challenging or doesn't go as planned, it's easy to look back at our past, our "Egypt," and remember it with rose-colored glasses. We forget the struggles and the bondage because our current situation feels uncertain or uncomfortable. Our Egypts might be past relationships that weren't healthy but provided a sense of comfort. They could be old jobs that were unfulfilling but felt secure. They might even be a way of life or a way of thinking that kept us stuck but felt predictable.

In moments of discomfort, we may find ourselves longing for what was rather than embracing what God is doing right now. We fail to recognize that God led us out of those situations for a reason—to bring us into a new season of growth, trust, and future promises.

Like the Israelites, we need to focus on the "manna" that God is providing in our lives right now. We must be grateful for the people, provisions, opportunities, and grace we have been given to press on another day. Remember, God didn't just bring the Israelites out of Egypt to leave them in the wilderness; he was leading them to the Promised Land. Likewise, God has promises for you, and while you walk toward those promises, he will supply you with everything you need.

Yet, if we do not actively remember who God is, we will passively forget all that God has done. This is why we must catch ourselves in moments of grumbling and start humbling ourselves before God. He is continuously pouring out his blessings and provision in our lives, but if we are too busy complaining, we might miss it.

Instead of romanticizing the past or longing for the comfort of our Egypts, let's embrace the manna God has given us today. Trust that each provision, no matter how small or unexpected, is a part of his perfect plan to lead us toward a promised future. Instead of complaining about the manna, give thanks to Hosanna.

Reflect

- Reflect on Exodus 16. How can you remember what God has done in your life?
- What parts of your past are you romanticizing? How can you focus on your "manna" instead of your "Egypts"?

Jesus, you're my provider, and I thank you for every blessing in my life. Help me to remember all you've done and to be grateful for all I have. May I not romanticize where I was but maintain hope for where you are leading me. In Jesus' name. Amen.

2

It's a Trap

I say then: Walk in the Spirit, and you shall not fulfill the lust of the flesh.

GALATIANS 5:16 NKJV

The Chinese finger trap was all the rage when I was a kid. Have you ever used one? These cylinder toys are woven from some kind of kung fu bamboo and can fill you with rage if you don't know how they work. I remember my first tussle with one.

I was sitting next to a classmate in the cafeteria, minding my ten-year-old business, when she handed me a little doodad with openings on each side. She giggled, told me to put my fingers inside, and watched eagerly. Curious, I obliged. It may come as no surprise that my phalanges were suddenly stuck in a vice grip! Laughter spilled out of my classmate's mouth as she watched me fight for my finger-loving life.

I pulled with all my might, but the trap only grew tighter. With my patience and circulation diminishing, I did the only thing I could think to do—I panicked. Then, like a wild honey badger, I began gnawing at the trap with my teeth. Fortunately, my friend stopped me before I ended up with splinters in my esophagus.

She explained that I had to stop pulling and instead push my fingers together. I did as she said, and after several moments of frustration, I was free! Instead of pulling away, I learned that the key to freedom was pressing in.

The same can be said for our walks with Jesus. When we press into God, we press into his freedom. Christ came to set us free from the bondage of sin and death so that in him we may have life and experience its fullness. However, sin predisposes us to self-reliance. Even though we may desire to live for God, we are constantly tempted to be led by our flesh.

In Galatians, the apostle Paul explains that the flesh and the Spirit are enemies to one another because they desire contrary things. The flesh desires what is natural, human, and opposed to God. The Spirit desires what is supernatural, divine, and of God. As believers, our lives are held in constant tension between the two. While we may be willing to walk in the Spirit and obey God, we will often feel tempted to do the opposite.

Walking in the flesh is like pulling on the finger trap. When we feel the pressures of being stuck in an uncomfortable environment, we naturally want to pull away from God toward the things of self, which only makes matters worse. The Spirit, on the other hand, calls us to move in a way that is opposite to our nature. God will draw us closer to himself and reveal that our way leads to bondage, but his way always leads to escape.

The Bible also reminds us that "those who live according to the flesh have their minds set on what the flesh desires; but those who live in accordance with the Spirit have their minds set on what the Spirit desires" (Romans 8:5 NIV). This passage further highlights the conflict between our fleshly impulses and our spiritual calling.

To walk in the Spirit means to fix our minds on the things of God and actively choose his ways over our own. When we set our minds on the Spirit, we experience life and peace, breaking free from the traps of the flesh that seek to hold us captive.

Life is full of difficulties, and hardship tends to highlight the areas in our hearts where we depend on God the least. When we fail to walk in the Spirit, we should not condemn ourselves but take it as an opportunity to reflect. We can ask our mighty Father in heaven how we can break free from the people, circumstances, habits, and mindsets that harm us.

No matter how often we are tempted to pull away, we can always press into the freedom that God has given us.

Reflect

- Read Galatians 5. Take a moment to reflect on the chapter and ask the Lord to reveal areas in your life where you can press into him more.
- Recall an experience where you felt trapped and tempted to pull away. How did you respond initially, and what did you learn from that experience?

Jesus, thank you for your freedom. In moments when I feel stuck, help me not to lean on myself but to depend on you instead. Help me press into the freedom found in your Spirit. In Jesus' name. Amen.

3

Pride Comes Before the...Leprosy

[Miriam and Aaron] said, "Has the LORD indeed spoken only through Moses? Has He not spoken through us also?"

NUMBERS 12:2 NKJV

When we hear the phrase "pride and prejudice," the classic Jane Austen novel by the same name may immediately come to mind. It's a story filled with characters who wrestle with their own biases and judgments, leading to misunderstandings and complications. But long before Elizabeth Bennet and Mr. Darcy made their complicated debut, there was another story of pride and prejudice—one that involved a chosen prophet named Moses and his siblings' rebellion against him. A rebellion that led them to face the consequences of conceit.

As the leader appointed by God to guide the Israelites, Moses had a unique line of direct communication with God, giving him unparalleled authority. His siblings, Aaron and Miriam, were also given significant roles: Aaron as Moses' spokesman and high priest, and Miriam as a prophetess and leader of the Israelite women. However, their pride led them to question Moses' leadership, particularly his decision to marry an Ethiopian woman, with the self-righteous claim, "Has the Lord spoken only through Moses? Hasn't he spoken through us, too?" (Numbers 12:2 NLT).

God, being the heavenly Father that he is, heard their boastful remarks and knew it was time for a serious reprimand. You know the kind—when a parent catches their child acting out of line and, through gritted teeth, commands them to "Come here now!" Well, that is precisely what happened next.

Descending in a cloud, God called them out, making it clear that Moses had a unique calling that should not be questioned. His anger burned against them, and when he left, Miriam was temporarily struck with leprosy. Ironically, criticizing someone else's skin caused Miriam to receive an affliction on her own—a stark reminder of the consequences of pride and prejudice. By questioning Moses' authority, Aaron and Miriam failed to recognize that they were also challenging God himself.

The story of Miriam and Aaron's rebellion against Moses is a powerful reminder of how sneaky pride can be. It often begins with a small, unspoken insecurity or a fleeting feeling of jealousy, but if left unchecked, it can quickly escalate into something more destructive.

In the case of Miriam and Aaron, Moses had done nothing wrong by marrying an Ethiopian woman, but Miriam and Aaron allowed underlying resentment toward Moses' relationship with God to grow roots of projected insecurity and prejudice. While in their case, this pride led to prejudice, in our own lives, it is often more likely to manifest as jealousy.

For instance, we may find ourselves criticizing a colleague's success, not because they've done anything wrong but because their achievements highlight our own insecurities. Perhaps a friend received an opportunity or recognition that we feel we deserved, and instead of celebrating their success, we harbor feelings of resentment or jealousy. This kind of pride sneaks in when we feel overlooked or undervalued, prompting us to question why others are being blessed while we seemingly are not. We may find ourselves motivated by jealousy, grumbling outwardly or inwardly about perceived injustice instead of leading with love and genuinely supporting others.

The good news is that God's love for us is unwavering, even when we struggle with pride and jealousy. When we recognize these feelings within ourselves, we have the opportunity to turn back to him, asking for his help to transform our hearts. As we surrender our pride and focus on God's faithfulness, we begin to see that our value is not diminished by the success of others, nor is God's ability to bless us limited by what he's doing in someone else's life.

Let's seek God's guidance and make a conscious effort to acknowledge and surrender any prideful perspectives we have. By doing so, we will not only strengthen our relationships with others but also deepen our relationship with God, experiencing a love that transcends pride and prejudice.

Reflect

- In what areas of your life do you struggle with feeling overlooked or undervalued, and how can you invite God to transform these feelings into humility and love?
- When you recognize feelings of pride or resentment, how do you typically respond? What steps can you take to align your heart more closely with God's will in those moments?

Heavenly Father, help me not to let pride or jealousy take root in me. Help me to grow in humility, and please minister to any places in my heart that feel overlooked. Thank you for seeing me and using me uniquely. In Jesus' name. Amen.

4

Windchill Moments

Those who trust in the LORD will renew their strength; they will soar on wings like eagles; they will run and not become weary, they will walk and not faint.

ISAIAH 40:31 CSB

It was January 2015, and our flight from Los Angeles had just landed in Detroit, Michigan. I looked through the small oval window and watched workers move across the tarmac while flurries of snow whirled in the air. It looked so cold, and something about the overcast sky resonated with the gloominess I felt in my heart.

Weeks prior to boarding that plane, my mom, grandpa, sister, and I stood around my sick grandma's hospital bed. She had been battling cancer for more than a year, and though we truly believed she would recover, she didn't. My strong, beautiful, hilariously funny grandma with a contagious laugh and a deep love for Jesus—she was gone. I wished we had boarded the flight with my healthy and healed grandma, but instead we were sadly on our way to attend her memorial service.

Eventually the pilot's muffled voice spoke over the intercom, "Ladies and gentlemen, welcome to Detroit,

Michigan, where the temperature is currently ten degrees with a windchill of negative twenty." I quickly looked at my grandpa in disbelief and asked him what on earth windchill was. My native-to-California ears had never heard such a thing.

My grandpa explained that windchill is not the actual temperature but what the temperature feels like when the wind hits your skin. Basically, the weather is cold, but it would feel even colder because of the wind. In hindsight, it perfectly describes that time of my life. I was in a "windchill" season, and I struggled to feel the warmth of God.

When my grandma was going through chemotherapy, I prayed fervently, fasted regularly, and believed God would make her well. But when the chilling sound of her flatlining monitor hit my ears, grief immediately filled my heart. I wasn't just broken by the loss of my grandma; I was devastated by the biting feeling that God wasn't there—that he had turned his back on us when we needed him most.

A man in the Bible named Job understood this feeling too. He lost everything: his children, his wealth, and his health. In anguish he said, "I cry out to you, God, but you do not answer; I stand up, but you merely look at me. You turn on me ruthlessly; with the might of your hand you attack me" (Job 30:20–21 NIV). Just like the windchill makes the temperature feel colder than it actually is, the winds of sorrow sometimes cause us to feel like God isn't there.

Job's cries were raw and real, much like our own when we face seasons of profound grief or disappointment. Yet, even in his despair, Job did something crucial: he continued to speak to God. He didn't turn away; instead, he brought his pain, confusion, and anger directly to the Lord.

In Job 23:3, he cries, "If only I knew where to find him; if only I could go to his dwelling!" (NIV). In the midst of suffering, Job still longed for God's presence. He understood that while he was overcome with feelings of heartache and sorrow, his feelings did not change the truth that God would never leave him.

When we are in the middle of our windchill moments, bracing ourselves against the icy sting of loss and the cold gusts of defeat, it can be tempting to withdraw from God. But it is precisely in these moments that we need him the most. Job's perseverance in pursuing God through the coldest moments of his life shows us that it is okay to struggle and express our pain to God. He will never abandon us and is big enough to carry our pain.

Winds may blow and the coldness of life may sting, but that never extinguishes the steady flame of God's love. He is with you, guiding you through every storm and enveloping you with the warmth of his presence.

Reflect

- When you find yourself in a windchill moment of life, how can you intentionally remind yourself of God's steadfast love?
- Take a moment today or this week to write down one promise from Scripture that reassures you of God's presence. How can you remind yourself of this when you feel overwhelmed?

Lord, thank you for your warming presence. When my heart is consumed with grief and I feel overcome by despair, keep my heart from hardening in the coldness of loss. Help me to cling to your Word and remember the truth that you will never abandon me, even in times when I feel alone. Comfort my heart, oh Lord, and remind me of your unfailing love. In Jesus' name. Amen.

5

Friendship Through the Roof

They came, bringing to him a paralytic carried by four men.

MARK 2:3 ESV

Have you ever heard the story "Footprints in the Sand"? It's a timeless poem that tells of a person who dreamed they were walking on the beach with the Lord. The beach represented life's journey. As the dreamer walked, they looked back over the path of their life and noticed that when times were good, there were two sets of footprints in the sand. But during times of struggle, there was only one set of footprints in the sand.

The dreamer questioned God because the single set of footprints implied that God had abandoned them during their greatest times of need. But the Lord gently replied, "My precious child, I love you and would never leave you. During your times of trial and suffering, when you see only one set of footprints, it was then that I carried you."[1]

---

1 Mary Stevenson, "Footprints in the Sand," 1939.

This heartfelt message reassures us of God's faithfulness and reminds us of the truth that God will provide us with whatever support we need to continue walking with him. Sometimes that support comes in the form of community—one that is willing to pick us up when we're too weak to do it ourselves.

The support of community is beautifully illustrated in the story of the paralyzed man found in Mark 2. Think of the hopelessness and frustration he must have felt when he knew healing was within reach, but he couldn't get himself there. Thankfully, this man had friends who reminded him that he didn't have to do it alone. Determined to get him to Jesus, who was inaccessible due to a large crowd, they hoisted their friend onto the roof above where Jesus was preaching.

Driven by loyalty and faith, the men dug through the roof and lowered their friend into the room on a mat. Seeing their faith, Jesus said, "Your sins are forgiven…I say to you, rise, pick up your bed, and go home" (Mark 2:5, 11 ESV). Immediately the man picked up his bed in front of everyone and left.

The story of the paralyzed man is a powerful reminder of how essential community can be in our walk of faith. Just as the man's friends carried him to Jesus, we, too, should strive to be the type of friends who do the same.

There are countless moments in life when people we love may feel paralyzed by fear, doubt, grief, or the weight of circumstances beyond their control. The Bible teaches us to bear one another's burdens in love (Galatians 6:2). That is what the paralyzed man's friends did. They recognized a friend in need and did not limit their encouragement to words. They took action, exemplifying a level of faith, loyalty, and love that we, as believers, should all aspire to. Their act of selfless love and determination showcases the power of true friendship.

But the story of the paralyzed man isn't just about being a friend who carries; it's also about recognizing when we need to be carried as well. When we begin to feel incapable of picking ourselves up, we may be tempted to retreat and self-isolate, especially if we've had painful experiences with others in the past.

Fear of being hurt again can lead us to build walls to keep the wrong people out, but doing so also prevents the right people from getting in. Instead of guarding our hearts in isolation, we can open them in faith to the right people who God brings into our lives. The right people are those who lift us up and carry us when we can't take another step. When we are willing to let down our walls a bit and admit when we are in need, we open the door for deep, life-giving relationships.

Maybe this level of community is something you have desired but have struggled to find. If this is a pain point in your life, remember that God cares about your deepest needs and can provide you with the friendships you need. He is faithful to bring the right people into your life, people who will pave the way for ongoing mutual support through life's highs and lows. Learning how to give *and* receive this level of support is a significant part of maturing in Christ.

When we allow ourselves to carry and be carried by others, we are not just leaning on human strength; we are also embracing God's provision through his people. God uses us to bring each other to him, to bear one another's burdens, and to ensure that no one has to walk—or be carried by God—alone.

Reflect

- Read Galatians 6:2. What does this verse mean to you and how can you apply it to your life?
- Do you find it easier to give or receive help from others? Why is that?

Lord, please provide me with a strong community. A community where I can offer support and be supported. Thank you for all the relationships you've already given me and the future relationships you will bring into my life. In Jesus' name. Amen.

6

YOUzzah Had Good Intentions

When they came to Nachon's threshing floor, Uzzah put out his hand to the ark of God and took hold of it, for the oxen stumbled. Then the anger of the Lord was aroused against Uzzah, and God struck him there for his error; and he died there by the ark of God.

2 SAMUEL 6:6–7 NKJV

Have you ever done something with the best of intentions, only to later reap a negative outcome? Maybe you were honest but accidentally hurt someone's feelings. Tried to break up a fight and ended up taking a punch. Attempted to surprise someone who, unbeknownst to you, happened to hate surprises. As much as we may dislike it, the truth is that good intentions don't always lead to good results. This is particularly illustrated through the story of Uzzah and the ark of the covenant.

In 2 Samuel 6, King David and thirty thousand men chosen from Israel were traveling to bring the ark of the covenant back to Jerusalem. The ark represented God's presence among the Israelites and was a physical manifestation of his covenant with them, so its return was a momentous occasion and cause for celebration. As the men celebrated, Uzzah and his brother Ahio, the men tasked with transporting the ark, drove the cart that carried it.

When the men arrived at the threshing floor of Nacon, one of the oxen leading the cart stumbled and the ark began to tip. Instinctively, Uzzah placed his hand on the ark to brace it from falling—a well-intentioned but disobedient act. After touching the ark, Uzzah was immediately struck down by God, and he died right there before the ark of God.

Now, you may find yourself wondering why on earth it was such a big deal to touch the ark. Did Uzzah really have to die over such a seemingly insignificant and well-intentioned decision? Well, to understand why Uzzah's action led to such a drastic outcome, we need to delve into the biblical significance of the ark of the covenant.

God's instructions on how the ark was to be handled were clear and explicit: it was to be carried using poles on the shoulders of the Levites, never touched by human hands (Numbers 4:15). Under the Old Covenant Law, the Israelites were required to follow God's commands precisely, especially regarding sacred objects like the ark of the covenant, the earthly throne of God. Any deviation from God's explicit instructions, even if well-intentioned, was a serious act of disobedience with severe consequences.

Based on this breakdown, Uzzah not only disobeyed God by touching the ark, but he also disobeyed God in their method of transporting it. Instead of carrying it on poles, he and his brother placed it on a cart to be hauled by oxen. They probably intended to lighten the physical load and speed up the journey, but their decision to disobey God in one way ultimately led Uzzah to disobey him in another.

Ironically, when Uzzah touched the ark, he was on the threshing floor, which in biblical context was a place where wheat was separated from the chaff. This is symbolic of our need to be set apart in holiness as believers.

Like Uzzah, sometimes our instincts lead us to disobedience. Even when we want to honor God, we might make decisions that lead to major consequences. Our well-intentioned but disobedient choices may not involve touching an ark, but they could be decisions like ignoring God's warning to end a relationship because we "just want to help the person" or continuing a certain habit because we "don't mean any harm" by it.

We might minimize the need to seek God's guidance in every decision, thinking that our intentions alone are enough to justify our actions.

However, the story of Uzzah reminds us that good intentions are not a substitute for obedience to God.

Thankfully, unlike Uzzah, we are covered by grace and have received the righteousness of God through Christ (2 Corinthians 5:21). This allows us to approach God's throne with boldness and, by the power of the Holy Spirit, discern between good intentions and true obedience.

As you reflect on today's message, think about where you might be relying on your intentions instead of seeking God's guidance. Praise God that his mercy is new every morning, and be sure to thank him for the marvelous grace *youzzah* now have.

Reflect

- How does the story of Uzzah challenge your understanding of obedience to God's commands?
- Consider the "touching the ark" moments in your life and the grace God has shown you. What do you think and feel about this?

Thank you, Jesus, for your divine grace and forgiveness. While my intentions may be good, I pray that by your Spirit, my actions will also be good in your sight. In Jesus' name. Amen.

7

It's a Lemon

"If any of you lacks wisdom, you should ask God, who gives generously to all without finding fault, and it will be given to you."

James 1:5 NIV

Her name was Bertha. A cherry red 2006 Chrysler PT cruiser (with a convertible roof I might add), and she was my first car. My father gifted her to me in my early twenties, which was such a blessing because I was a broke college student, and buying a car was not in my budget.

After about a month of driving, my sweet ride became a sour lemon. Anything that could possibly go wrong with a car seemed to go wrong with mine: Axle broken, engine replaced, air conditioning busted, brakes out. Once, an entire wheel flew off the car while I was driving! Clearly the Lord was with me and keeping me safe because Bertha, who I renamed Broke-Down Bertha, was trying to take my life *and* deplete my bank account. Before I knew it, I had spent more money fixing Bertha than my father paid to buy her.

Eventually I realized I had been making a poor investment and would have been better off saving for a new car. The problem was that I had yet to understand the concept of sunken cost, which is the money, time, and effort already spent that cannot be recovered.

Just like my endless investment in Broke-Down Bertha, sometimes we pour our resources into relationships, circumstances, or habits that we shouldn't. Instead of letting go and moving on, we are tempted to hold on because we have already invested so much. Despite all evidence of the contrary, we might hold on to the hope that things will eventually turn around if we just keep trying. Our ability to see potential can blind us to reality, causing us to sink in a sea of cost if we aren't careful.

Yet, as Ecclesiastes 3:6 explains, there is a "time to search and a time to give up, a time to keep and a time to throw away." We may care deeply about a person, project, or passion, but sometimes the wisest thing to do is recognize when our investment holds no value and move on. It may feel like we have wasted our resources by moving on, but in reality, we are simply making a new investment in our future.

Eventually, someone rear-ended Bertha and insurance deemed the damage a total loss. In all honesty, it was a blessing in disguise. God used the collision to change my circumstances, and I was able to use the insurance money as a down payment on a new car. In the same way, our inability to walk away will sometimes lead us to a wreck, but thankfully God wastes nothing.

God is faithful to help us recognize where we invest ourselves and what does not bear fruit. In John 15:2 Jesus says, "He cuts off every branch in me that bears no fruit, while every branch that does bear fruit he prunes so that it will be even more fruitful." This reminds us that God wants us to be fruitful, and he desires that we see a good return on our investments of time, energy, and resources.

Worldly investments can fail us, but investing in Jesus always leads to peace, patience, and fulfillment. Alongside that, it guarantees a return that is eternal. That is why we need to store up our treasures in heaven (Matthew 6:19–20). Investing in Jesus is the best investment we can make, and we can trust that an investment held in God's hands is better than an investment held in our own.

If we are willing to let go and let God show us where to put our time and energy, we can have peace of mind, knowing that our resources have not been wasted. Whenever we are tempted to continue holding on to promises of potential, let us remind ourselves of the promises of God.

Let's ask God for the wisdom to know when it is time for us to surrender and to help us discern when something is a lemon.

Reflect

- What specific things do you need to let go of and place in God's hands?
- How can you actively trust God with these areas?

Jesus, help me recognize any poor investments I may be making. Fill me with the discernment to know when something is a lemon and the courage to move on. In Jesus' name. Amen.

8

Well, That Was Refreshing

"Whoever drinks of the water that I will give him will never be thirsty again. The water that I will give him will become in him a spring of water welling up to eternal life."

John 4:14 ESV

We all have places we retreat to when we're feeling overwhelmed. The cozy chair in the corner, the quiet trail where we can clear our thoughts, or that one spot with a view so beautiful it makes the world go still.

For one Samaritan woman, her retreat was a well in Samaria. The well was more to her than just a place to draw water; it was a refuge from the whispers and judgmental stares of the town that labeled her an outcast. She also knew that the best time to visit the well was whenever she could be alone. Her plan worked perfectly, until one day she met a man at the well who didn't just see her—he saw right through her. A man named Jesus.

In order to understand the significance of encountering a Jewish man like Jesus at a Samaritan well, it is important to know that Jews and Samaritans had a long history of tension. The Jews considered the Samaritans a mixed race (Samaritans had come from the intermarriages between Israelites and foreigners after the Assyrian conquest), and they deemed Samaritan religious practices impure. For those reasons, Jews typically avoided interactions with Samaritans, especially one with this woman's reputation.

But Jesus, unconcerned with such pretenses and tired from his journey to Galilee, stopped at the well in Samaria to rest his body. Ultimately though, his purpose was to refresh the soul of this Samaritan woman. Jesus asked her for a drink, to which she answered, "You are a Jew and I am a Samaritan woman. How can you ask me for a drink?" (John 4:9 NIV). He explained to her, "Everyone who drinks this water will be thirsty again, but whoever drinks the water I give them will never thirst. Indeed, the water I give them will become in them a spring of water welling up to eternal life" (vv. 4:13–14 NIV).

The woman had come to the well to satisfy a physical need, yet Jesus offered her something to quench the thirst of her soul. He, an obvious stranger to her, further revealed that he knew her past: "You have had five husbands, and the man you now have is not your husband" (v. 18 NIV). And Jesus wasn't just calling out the sin of the Samaritan woman; he was addressing a deeper unmet need in her heart that led her to sin in the first place.

The Samaritan woman's response wasn't one of defensiveness but amazement: "'Sir,' the woman said, 'I can see that you are a prophet'" (v. 19 NIV). As their conversation continued, the Samaritan woman realized that Jesus was no ordinary man—he was the Messiah.

Deeply moved, the woman left behind her bucket (a symbol of her old life) and ran back to the town to tell everyone about her divine encounter with Jesus. She was radically transformed, and by the power of her testimony, many in the community were changed as well.

The beautiful thing about this interaction is that Jesus saw the insatiable longing for love within the Samaritan woman's heart, a yearning that left her dry and searching for more. He looked beyond her outward behavior and understood the very core of who she was. As 1 Samuel 16:7 reads, "People look at the outward appearance, but the Lord looks at the heart" (NIV). In turn, Jesus offered her himself, the living water that would eternally quench her thirst with endless love.

The Samaritan woman's story is a powerful reminder that if we allow Jesus to reach into the hidden places of our hearts and see us completely, he will expose areas of sin and quench the unmet thirsts of our hearts. He doesn't just offer temporary relief, he offers lasting transformation.

When we are tempted to retreat to our wells of shame, let us remember that no matter where we've been or what we've done, Jesus meets us with both truth and grace, offering something greater than what we've been searching for: living water that truly satisfies.

Reflect

- Even if it is subtle, where are you seeking fulfillment outside of Jesus?
- What are some of the "wells" in your life? How can you encounter Jesus in that space and allow him to minister to the deepest places in your heart?

Lord, reveal unmet needs in my heart. Thank you for meeting me in my wells of shame and bringing me a sense of acceptance. May I allow your living water to satisfy my soul and transform my life. In Jesus' name. Amen.

9

The Reformer

The Lord *is good to those whose hope is in him, to the one who seeks him; it is good to wait quietly for the salvation of the* Lord*.*

Lamentations 3:25–26 NIV

People who attend regular Pilates classes are called "Pilates Warriors" for a reason. These mighty people willingly suit up in their LuLu armor, pull up their grippy socks, and subject themselves to an hour of excruciating pain, sometimes daily.

Years ago, one of my Pilates Warrior friends invited me to join her. Now, as a former athlete and a regular gym goer, I assumed I would be ready for the class. Let's just say that nothing could have prepared my muscles for that experience.

At the start of class, we all found our way to a Reformer machine. If you've never seen a Reformer, it looks like it belongs in a medieval dungeon. The machine is about seven feet long, resembles a bed frame, and has a cushioned platform in the center that glides back and forth on metal tracks. It also comes complete with resistance springs, pulleys, straps, handles, and a foot bar.

With the enthusiasm of a professional cheerleader, the instructor guided us through a series of exercises. As if the movements themselves weren't challenging enough, we were also told to hold our bodies in difficult positions for what felt like an eternity. My body was quaking like the Quaker Oats man, but I held each position as instructed.

A small—okay large—part of me wanted to demand the instructor to move on to the next exercise. But I remained in place because I understood that the pain was a sign that my muscles were engaging in ways I wasn't used to. Similarly, when God calls us to stillness and tells us to remain where we are, it sometimes starts to feel like we have been in that place for far too long. It can be incredibly frustrating, especially when we have faithfully followed God's instructions and feel ready for his next move.

When the Lord calls us to remain in a position longer than we desire, we should not resent his process. He understands what the brain and body need and knows exactly how to strengthen his children at the core. As Psalm 46:10 reminds us, "Be still, and know that I am God." We may exercise our faith regularly, but the deepest spiritual muscles are often activated in stillness.

It is in stillness that we discover a deeper trust and reliance on God's strength. It is in stillness that we learn to surrender our need for control and submit to

God's perfect timing and wisdom. Psalm 37:7 reminds us, "Be still before the LORD and wait patiently for him; do not fret when people succeed in their ways, when they carry out their wicked schemes."

The reformer of life experience can stretch us beyond our comfort zone and throw us off balance, but the guidance of the Lord brings stability. In Exodus 14:14, the Israelites were told, "The LORD will fight for you; you need only to be still." Sometimes, God's greatest work in us happens when we cease striving and allow him to move on our behalf.

Being still isn't about inactivity; it's about a posture of the heart that trusts in God's sovereignty. It's about letting go of our fears and anxieties, knowing that he is at work even when we can't see it. It is often in these times of stillness and waiting that God prepares us for the next step, molding our character and deepening our faith so that when the time comes to move, we do so with renewed strength and purpose.

It is possible that God is telling you to hold your position in this moment. You may have to remain at that job, maintain a status of singleness, hold on for a breakthrough, or continue to wait for the right opportunity. James 1:4 encourages us, "Let perseverance finish its work so that you may be mature and complete, not lacking anything."

Whatever position God is holding you in, remind yourself that there is power in the pause. Even in our weakness, holding on to the instruction of the Lord will always bring us strength.

Reflect

- What position is God calling you to remain in right now?
- What challenges do you face when God calls you to stay in a place longer than you desire, and how can you continue to trust him during that time?

Father, help me to wait on you and trust the power you bring in the pause. Thank you for revealing my weakness and strengthening me in stillness. Teach me how to hold fast to your instruction and exercise my faith in new ways. In Jesus' name. Amen.

10

A Lot with a Little

Andrew, Simon Peter's brother, spoke up. "There's a young boy here with five barley loaves and two fish. But what good is that with this huge crowd?"

JOHN 6:8–9 NLT

Do you ever wonder if what you do matters? Do you ever wonder if *you* matter? In a world as vast as ours, it's easy to question our significance. Yet, just as a small pebble can cause a major ripple in a pond, God can do extraordinary things with whatever we bring to him, even if we believe it isn't enough. The disciples learned this firsthand.

One day, the disciples were sitting with Jesus when thousands of hungry people started walking toward them. Jesus turned to his disciple Philip and, as a test, asked him where they should buy enough bread to feed the crowd. As many of us would, the disciples reacted with doubt and skepticism.

Philip explained that it would take half a year's salary to buy enough bread to feed even a nibble to each person. Another disciple, Andrew, pointed out a young boy who had five loaves of bread and two fish, but Andrew questioned the value of such a small amount of food and certainly didn't consider it helpful.

Soon, all twelve disciples approached Jesus and said, "Send the people away so that they can go to the surrounding countryside and villages and buy themselves something to eat" (Mark 6:36 NIV). In other words, "Let the people feed themselves because that is *not* our job." Of course they didn't have enough money or food to feed the masses, and it didn't make sense for them to take on the responsibility of feeding five thousand people on such short notice.

Jesus instructed the disciples to have all the people sit down. Then he took the bread and fish, gave thanks, and distributed the pieces among the people. After everyone had eaten, twelve baskets of leftovers remained.

This story reminds us of the powers of both perception and provision. When faced with feeding the multitude, the disciples immediately focused on what they *didn't* have; they viewed their situation through a lens of lack and limitation instead of remembering that they were with a limitless God. How often do we adopt the same mindset, focusing on whatever we perceive we lack instead of focusing on God's profound power?

Jesus offers us a different perspective. When he took what little was offered (the five loaves and two fish), he didn't focus on the lack of resources; instead, he gave thanks for everything the Father had already provided.

Imagine the ripple effect your life can have on the world around you if you commit to thinking like Jesus, allowing his transformative power to overflow from within. Because just like Christ, our lives can inspire others to triumph over fear, walk by faith in the face of doubt, seek solace in God's presence, and take action through prayer. Thinking like Jesus leads us to live like Jesus—and that leads to abundance only God can give.

Although we have been blessed with the mind of Christ (1 Corinthians 2:16), we, much like the disciples, sometimes rely on logic and reason instead of biblical truth and faith. Instead of adopting the mind of Christ, we adopt the mind of self. And when we cling to our limited human understanding, we run the risk of gradually doubting God's power of provision and becoming jaded. But what if we shifted our mindset from one of lack and instead asked ourselves, *What can God do with all that I already have?*

Our areas of lack are not obstacles; they're opportunities for God to demonstrate his might. No matter how small or insignificant we may believe something to be, even if that something is ourselves, God can certainly use it for his abundant purpose. We must remove our scarcity mindset and put on the mind of Christ, giving God our "not enough" and trusting that, in time, he will provide more than enough. He is not limited by human constraints because he is a supernatural and limitless God.

The disciples may have seen only five loaves and two fish, but Jesus saw the possibility for so much more. He sees the same for you and will create ripples of impact through your willingness to serve, to give, and to love.

So, today, move forward with confidence, knowing that in the hands of our God, we lack no good thing. Every act of kindness, every word of encouragement, every small step of faith matters. You matter.

Reflect

- Think of a time when you felt you didn't have enough of something. How did this belief impact your actions or decisions?
- How can you change your perspective to see challenges as opportunities for God to demonstrate his power?

Father, help me to surrender a scarcity mindset. May I always remember that with you I lack nothing. Thank you for everything you provide. In Jesus' name. Amen.

11

Don't Knock Your Blessings

The Lord *opened the donkey's mouth, and she asked Balaam, "What have I done to you that you have beaten me these three times?"*

Numbers 22:28 CSB

The Bible has 1,189 chapters, sixty-six books, two testaments, and one story that always leaves me with a deeper appreciation for donkeys: the story of Balaam in Numbers 22.

King Balak of Moab sent messengers to ask Balaam, a prophet for hire, to curse the Israelites. God told Balaam not to return to Moab with Balak's messengers because the Israelites were blessed. Balaam obeyed, but then King Balak sent higher ranking messengers and promised even greater rewards.

Balaam was intrigued by Balak's offer and asked God again if he could go to Moab. God allowed Balaam to go but gave him strict instructions to say only what God told him to say. Eager to claim his reward, Balaam hopped on his donkey, unaware that God had different plans for him down the road.

During their travels, Balaam's donkey saw a powerful angel of the Lord standing in the way of their path and holding a drawn sword. Like any donkey with common sense, she turned off the path and into a field. Unable to see the angel, Balaam, filled with fury, beat the donkey. On two other occasions when the donkey saw the angel again, Balaam beat the donkey for going off course or causing a delay: once after she crushed his foot while she walked through a narrow passage made of stone walls and once after the donkey laid down under him.

Then, in a peculiar turn of events, God opened the donkey's mouth and gave her the ability to speak: "What have I done to you that you have beaten me these three times?" she asked. So blinded by rage, Balaam the Beater was not even fazed that his donkey was talking.

It was only after God opened Balaam's eyes to see the angel standing in the way that Balaam's demeanor changed. The angel explained that if the donkey had not turned away, he would have killed Balaam and spared the donkey. Balaam was so fixated on future rewards that he missed the blessing right in front of him. Without his donkey, he would not have survived.

By now, you may be wondering, as I did, why God gave Balaam permission to go in the first place, only to send an angel to stop him. In Numbers 22, we learn that God was angry with Balaam for going at all. God told him he *could* go, not that he *should* go. Balaam's decision revealed his true motivations: greed. His heart was torn between obedience to God and financial gain. While rather unconventional, God used the angel and the talking donkey to get through to Balaam's boorish brain and correct his heart.

This story teaches an important lesson for every believer: don't despise your detours. How often do we wind up doing *exactly* that? How often do we grumble because our life isn't going the way we think it should? If we know that his promises are yes and amen (2 Corinthians 1:20), why do we grow angry when we have to wait and hold on? If we believe our blessings are in him, why do we lash out when those blessings don't come fast enough?

Think of moments when things didn't go as planned—delayed flights, breakups, missed opportunities, denied loans. Is it possible that those were not just a series of unfortunate events but divine detours? Perhaps the setbacks in your life were actually setups for future success and protection from unseen dangers.

The truth is, we often perceive life as a means to a destination, and we fix our sights on reaching a point of reward. In reality, the true reward is in the journey itself. Instead of rushing to our goals and despising our detours, let's rest with our Father and trust his timing. Like Balaam, God may use the thing we least expect to correct our heart's posture.

Next time you face an unexpected turn in your journey, remember who you're on the journey with. Sometimes our obstacles are opportunities for God to show us something we could not see without them. He sees what you do not but may reveal those things to you in time. Enjoy the scenic route with God, and don't knock your blessings, especially when they come disguised as detours.

Reflect

- Read Numbers 22:21–35. How does Balaam's story change your view of life's detours?
- How do you usually react when things don't go as planned? What can you do to see those moments as potential blessings?

Father, help me to trust your timing and to see blessings in the detours of my life. Open my eyes to your guidance and teach me to embrace with faith and thanks whatever journey you set me on. In Jesus' name. Amen.

12

Cana Get an Amen?

When the wine ran out, the mother of Jesus said to him, "They have no wine." And Jesus said to her, "Woman, what does this have to do with me? My hour has not yet come." His mother said to the servants, "Do whatever he tells you."

JOHN 2:3–5 ESV

Weddings can be such beautiful and joyous occasions. From watching the bride walk down the aisle to shoulder bumping on the dance floor, weddings, when done right, are incredibly fun. Weddings of today can be grand, but not many compare to weddings of biblical times.

In biblical times, weddings weren't just private family affairs; they were public events that could last for several days. Weddings were also deeply connected to a family's honor, which meant the stakes were high for the hosts. Failure to plan well could bring devastating shame to the family, so it's no surprise that running out of wine would most certainly leave a lasting social stain. This is exactly what happened at a wedding at Cana in Galilee.

Jesus, the disciples, and Jesus' mother, Mary, were in attendance at the wedding in Cana when Mary realized the wine had run out. Her immediate reaction was to find Jesus and ask for his help. Jesus turned to her and said, "Woman, what does this have to do with me? My hour has not yet come" (John 2:4).

Seemingly ignoring Jesus' response, an undeterred Mary proceeded to command the servants to do whatever Jesus instructed, which led to Jesus performing the first miracle of his ministry: turning water into wine.

When thinking about this story, many focus on Jesus' miraculous act, but the account of the wedding at Cana also teaches us the importance of intercession. Intercession is recognizing the needs, concerns, or challenges of others and approaching God in prayer to plead for help on their behalf. Mary interceded on behalf of the wedding hosts' need by bringing the need for more wine to Jesus. She understood something crucial: that Jesus is able to fulfill every need.

We, too, can intercede on behalf of people, organizations, leaders, and nations. Instead of recognizing a need and leaving it for someone else to deal with or feeling pressured to fix it ourselves, we can confidently bring the need to Jesus.

Like Mary, we are called to trust that Jesus will act, even when we feel uncertain about what to do next, even when his timing or methods are not immediately clear to us.

And just as the servants at Cana were told to follow Jesus' commands, we, too, are called to listen to his voice and act according to his guidance. Our role is not to dictate the outcome but to trust his wisdom and power to meet the need in his perfect way, knowing he always stands ready to step into our situation and turn it around.

When we intercede, we align ourselves with God's will, allowing his power to work through us and the situations we bring to his attention. We become part of his miraculous work, witnessing firsthand how he transforms lack into abundance and sorrow into joy. We act in faith with the understanding that his promises are always yes and amen.

Remember, Jesus has compassion for our needs. Whether our concern is about a friend who recently lost their job, a community rebuilding from a natural disaster, or a need for more wine at a reception, nothing is too big or too small for our God!

God cares about every detail of our lives and the lives of those we care about. He invites us to bring everything to him in prayer, so let us do so confidently! Let's make it a daily practice to bring our concerns and the needs of others to Jesus, trusting that he knows exactly what to do.

Reflect

- What practical steps can we take to ensure we regularly pray for others?
- Think of a time when someone interceded for you. How did it impact you?

Lord, build me up as an intercessor. Open my eyes to see a spiritual need and teach me to use prayer to war on others' behalf. In Jesus' name. Amen.

13

Too Good to Be True

"A thief comes only to steal and kill and destroy. I have come so that they may have life and have it in abundance."

John 10:10 CSB

Have you ever found yourself in a season of life when everything seems to be going right? You've landed that dream job, formed meaningful relationships, or achieved a long-held goal. Blessings seem to pour in abundantly, but right when you start settling in and enjoying the moment, an unsettling thought creeps in: *What if something bad is about to happen?* Suddenly your peace is challenged, your blessings feel fleeting, and your heart is consumed with worry that all of that good is simply too good to be true.

In psychology, this experience is known as catastrophizing—an anxious habit where we anticipate the worst, even when things are going well. The tendency to catastrophize is often seen as a maladaptive defense mechanism and one that causes more harm than good. This habit of mentally preparing for the worst-case scenario can result from a litany of things: past trauma, perfectionism, learned behaviors from our upbringing, or ongoing stress.

Psychologists may consider catastrophizing a cognitive distortion, but we, as believers, recognize it as the nagging voice of the Enemy trying to steal our peace. Jesus warned us about this in John 10:10, reminding us that while the Enemy comes to steal, kill, and destroy, Jesus has come to give us life—life in abundance.

The voice of doubt, which urges us to expect the worst, is the Enemy's attempt to derail us from the abundant life Jesus promises. The Enemy knows that if he can plant seeds of fear and anxiety in our minds, he can distract us from the truth of God's blessings. He wants us to focus on everything that can go wrong rather than on the goodness and faithfulness of God. If he succeeds at causing us to ruminate on potential threats, he can rob us of our ability to enjoy the promises currently being fulfilled in our lives.

But something every believer has to understand is this: not every thought that enters our mind is our own. We have to discern the source of our thoughts and take captive any mindset that is not aligned with the truth of God's Word. The Bible tells us, "We destroy arguments and every lofty opinion raised against the knowledge of God, and take every thought captive to obey Christ" (2 Corinthians 10:5 ESV). Through the help of the Holy Spirit, we have the power to tell the devil to "shut up and sit down" by rejecting every thought that is not from God and depending on what we know to be true.

While the Enemy wants us to expect the worst, we serve a God who gives us the best. Jeremiah 29:11 reassures us, "For I know the plans I have for you, declares the LORD, plans for welfare and not for evil, to give you a future and a hope" (ESV). This verse reminds us that God's intentions toward us are always good, and his plans are designed to prosper us, not to harm us.

When the voice of the Enemy sounds too loud to ignore, we can tune out his nagging by practicing two key disciplines: gratitude and praise. Psalm 100:4 tells us to "enter his gates with thanksgiving, and his courts with praise! Give thanks to him; bless his name!" (ESV). When our minds are full of thanksgiving and praise, we leave no room for discontentment or condemnation. We shift our focus from what could go wrong to what has already gone right.

Gratitude grounds us in the present and reminds us of the ways God has been faithful throughout our lives. It reminds us that no matter what the future holds, God is the one holding our future. And when we begin to praise God for this faithfulness, we send a bold message to the Enemy that his efforts to derail our faith are futile. Through praise, we invite God's presence into our lives, and fear and doubt cannot stand in his presence.

So, in moments when doubt and fear try to overshadow our blessings, we can confidently turn to gratitude and praise, knowing these practices align our hearts with God's truth. We silence the Enemy's lies when we focus on God's faithfulness and declare his goodness, allowing us to fully embrace the abundant life Jesus promises. Trusting in God's plans, we can rest assured that his intentions for us are never too good to be true.

Reflect

- How can you focus on God's faithfulness instead of potential fears?
- How can you incorporate more gratitude and praise into your daily routine?

Lord, thank you for your abundant blessings. Help me to have a heart of thanks and a posture of praise. In Jesus' name. Amen.

14

Feelin' a Little Salty

Lot's wife looked back and became a pillar of salt.
GENESIS 19:26 CSB

Let's talk about Lot and the saltiest woman in the Bible, formerly known as Lot's wife. You know, the woman who infamously disobeyed instructions to not look back at Sodom and Gomorrah and, as a result, turned into a pillar of salt.

Since the Bible does not specify her name, maybe we can go with Mrs. Morton for today. That seems fitting. To keep things "kosher," let's add a bit of context to the story by taking a deeper look at the events leading up to this "morton-fying" moment.

The cities of Sodom and Gomorrah were known for their wickedness and sin. Fewer than ten people *didn't* practice evil (Genesis 18:32). They were so full of wickedness that God decided he would pour out his judgment on the people.

But first, two angels descended and said to Lot, who lived in Sodom, "Do you have anyone else here—sons-in-law, sons or daughters, or anyone else in the city who belongs to you? Get them out of here, because we are going to destroy this place. The outcry to the Lord against its people is so great that he has sent us to destroy it" (Genesis 19:12–13 NIV).

Afterward, Lot and his family were given clear instructions to flee for their lives and not look back. If they did, they would be destroyed right along with the cities. The two angels (whom the townspeople literally tried to mob against and assault, mind you) had just warned Lot and his family to flee, but instead of responding with urgency, they hesitated. The angels had to grab them by their hands and lead them out of the city.

Just when it seemed they had escaped, Mrs. Morton looked back. She did exactly what she was told *not* to do. Regardless of her reasoning, her poor decision turned her into seasoning, which was unfortunate. Eventually, Lot and the rest of his family got away and made it safely to the city of Zoar. Once they were there, God rained down burning sulfur on Sodom and Gomorrah, destroying all the vegetation and all the land.

Reading the story of Lot and his wife gives me the same feeling as when I watch an intense movie where the main character keeps making foolish decisions. I want to yell, "No! What are you doing?" into the pages of my Bible. However, while I am tempted to judge Lot and his family harshly, I have to remind myself that sometimes things are much easier said than done. The cities were morally corrupt, but they were also the cities that Lot and his family called home. Everyone and everything they knew was there, and I imagine they felt overwhelmed having to suddenly leave it all behind.

This story also teaches us a lot about the dangers of being too attached to the past and too comfortable with sin. Consider this verse: "This means that anyone who belongs to Christ has become a new person. The old life is gone; a new life has begun!" (2 Corinthians 5:17 NLT). Like Mrs. Morton, we might find comfort in corruption because it is familiar. We live in a fallen world, and the pull of our past can be strong, but God calls us to live new lifestyles.

We learn from Lot and his wife's story that disobedience leads to destruction, while obedience, on the other hand, leads to development. The act of turning away from sin is not a one-time event; it's an ongoing process. Each of us will be tempted to look back at the symbolic Sodoms in our lives. And whether we're tempted by jealousy, pride, sexual impurity, unforgiveness, or rage, each of us has something we must turn away from.

The process of learning to turn away from sin requires us to be open and honest both with ourselves and with God about the temptations we face. And when our Mrs. Morton tendencies act up and we turn toward sin, we can redirect our focus back to God.

With daily prayer, we can ask the Lord to help us let go of whatever corrupts our walk with him.

God's plans for us are forward-moving, leading us toward a life filled with his purpose and grace. With his provision and guidance, we find the strength to leave the past behind and embrace the future he has for us. And that is nothing to be salty about.

Reflect

- Read Genesis 18:16–19:29. What stands out to you most?
- What things from your past are you struggling to let go of? How do those attachments affect your spiritual walk?

Jesus, help me not turn back to sinful habits. Strengthen me in you and help me walk without hesitation into all you have for me. In Jesus' name. Amen.

15

Un-Baal-ievable

At noon Elijah began to taunt them. "Shout louder!" he said. "Surely he is a god! Perhaps he is deep in thought, or busy, or traveling. Maybe he is sleeping and must be awakened."

1 KINGS 18:27 NIV

Let's talk about one of the most epic showdowns in the Bible. No, it's not David versus Goliath or even Moses versus Pharaoh. This one involves a prophet, 450 false prophets, and a whole lot of water. You know the story of Elijah and the prophets of Baal on Mount Carmel (1 Kings 18:16–40). Picture it: a lone prophet squaring off against Baal's bonehead buddies. And what happens? Well, let's just say Elijah brings the fire, both literally and figuratively.

Elijah lived in a time when Israel had strayed far from God's ways (which, if we're being honest, was pretty much on-brand for Israel, so are we really surprised to learn about this piece of history?). The people turned away from God Almighty and were no longer driven by the faith of their ancestors. Instead, they were swayed by the allure of idolatry and began worshiping a Canaanite god. They believed that this pagan god called Baal could control the weather and bring prosperity, but all he brought was dust and despair.

The Israelites had lost their way *and* their minds. Under the corrupt leadership of King Ahab and his notorious Queen Jezebel, Israel was immersed in idolatry. But Elijah was prepared to do something about it. Fed up with the nonsense, he planned a divine duel between the false prophets and him. Each side would prepare a sacrifice, and the true God would reveal himself by sending fire from heaven. The stakes couldn't have been higher; it was life and death.

The prophets of Baal spent hours frantically dancing around their sacrificial altar. Their voices grew hoarse from shouting, and they marked their bodies with self-inflicted wounds in an attempt to get their god's attention. They were desperate; Elijah was amused. He stood back, watching and laughing at their failed efforts, and started mocking them. "Shout louder!" he said. "Maybe he's on a trip, or maybe he's taking a nap!" I can almost envision him stifling a laugh as he egged on the prophets.

When it was Elijah's turn, he didn't just prepare the sacrifice; he ordered that water be poured over the altar until everything was drenched. The sacrifice was so soaked that the only way it could catch fire was if God himself ignited the flame. Elijah prayed a simple prayer and BOOM! Fire fell from heaven, consuming the sacrifice, the wood, the stones, the water—everything.

And Elijah's story didn't end with the fire on Mount Carmel. After God's powerful display, the people fell to their knees, proclaiming, "The Lord—he is God! The Lord—he is God!" (1 Kings 18:39 NIV). The nation was brought back to the true God, and the rain that had been withheld for years finally began to fall again—a sign of God's mercy and restoration.

Even though Queen Jezebel had been killing prophets of Yahweh throughout the land, Elijah put himself on the line anyway to challenge the prophets of Baal. He knew this showdown was about reclaiming the hearts of a fallen nation, and his actions were driven by his profound, unwavering faith that God would reveal himself. Elijah had jokes *and* great confidence in God.

Elijah's faith and boldness weren't born out of arrogance; they were the result of a deep and unshakable trust in God. He didn't believe God *might* show up; he knew God *would* show up, and he was willing to stake it all on his conviction. This kind of "Godfidence," as we might call it, is a powerful reminder that when we step out in faith, God doesn't just meet us halfway—he goes above and beyond, showing up in ways that leave no room for doubt.

As you reflect on Elijah's story, ask yourself, *Where is God calling me to step out in faith? In what areas of my life do I need to trust God to bring the fire?* Let this story inspire you to step out in faith, even when the odds seem impossible, and believe that God will honor your commitment to him. Remember, when God shows up, he shows up in a big way—consuming doubts, fears, and obstacles that stand in our way—and leaving behind a testimony of his faithfulness that others cannot ignore.

Reflect

- Read 1 Kings 18:16–39. What stood out to you in Elijah's actions and attitude?
- What "soaked wood" situations in your life do you need to trust God with?
- Where is God calling you to step out in faith—to take that bold, seemingly irrational step that goes against all human logic?

Lord, help me to have the confidence of Elijah, trusting that you will show up in my life even when the odds seem impossible. May I always turn to you, knowing that you are the true God who answers by fire. In Jesus' name. Amen.

16

Feeling Puzzled

We know that all things work together for the good of those who love God, who are called according to his purpose.

Romans 8:28 CSB

Have you ever tried to put together a jigsaw puzzle without looking at the picture on the box? What starts as a simple task soon becomes a daunting challenge of sorting through hundreds of scattered pieces.

Without the reference image on the box, it's nearly impossible to determine where each piece belongs or what the final picture is meant to look like. Instead of an enjoyable experience, putting the puzzle together becomes incredibly frustrating.

Life has a way of feeling like an unsolved puzzle sometimes, doesn't it? We begin sorting through the pieces of our lives—career paths, relationships, experiences—while trying to make sense of them all. Each piece holds significance, yet without seeing the bigger picture, it's easy to feel overwhelmed and confused. We wonder how everything will come together—or if it ever will.

In times of confusion and frustration, it's essential to remember that God sees the complete picture of our lives. We may only hold a small, seemingly insignificant piece, but God knows exactly where it fits within his grand design.

Romans 8:28 reassures us that "all things work together for the good of those who love God, who are called according to his purpose." This verse is exemplified through the life of Joseph, whose story is one of the most profound examples of God's ability to fit together the scattered pieces of our lives into a beautiful picture.

Joseph's life was filled with events that, at first glance, seem disconnected. He was favored by his father, given a coat of many colors, and prophetically gifted in interpreting dreams. His future was set up to be bright—at least until he was betrayed by his brothers, thrown into a pit, and sold into slavery. While he maintained his faith and continued to honor God, one can only imagine the emotional pain he suffered because of those pieces, those life events. Yet God's favor was still upon him.

After being sold, Joseph was sent to serve a man named Potiphar. Over time, Joseph earned a position of trust in Potiphar's household. Perhaps in this moment Joseph could see the pieces of God's promises coming together. All *seemed* well…until Potiphar's wife made advances toward him. Joseph refused her, so Potiphar's wife falsely accused him of assaulting her. As a result, Joseph was imprisoned.

While imprisoned, Joseph interpreted the dreams of his fellow prisoners, and his interpretations of those dreams ultimately led him to interpret the dreams of the king. Each piece of Joseph's puzzle came to him years apart and seemingly from completely different puzzles, but each piece—each experience of his life—was essential in positioning and preparing him to serve as second in command over all of Egypt. His pieces had been divinely arranged into a purposeful picture.

Joseph's journey is a powerful reminder that the pieces of our lives—whether they are moments of joy or pain—are all part of a much larger picture that only God can see.

When we're holding onto pieces of our lives, we may grow discouraged by what we do or don't yet see. We may ask ourselves why nothing seems to fit, exhausting ourselves trying to arrange individual pieces, and then we grow frustrated when key pieces seem to be missing. We may fail to understand how any of the pieces will ever come together to become something good. If we aren't careful, we will eventually rely on our own vision more than God's.

Our hearts may plan the way, but God establishes each of our steps. And, just like a puzzle, our lives will come together one piece at a time. So, when you're feeling overwhelmed or puzzled by the events in your life, hold onto the truth of Romans 8:28 that "all things work together for the good of those who love God."

Even when you are unsure about the image of your life, remember that God created the reference image on the puzzle box of your life. He knows where every piece, relationship, experience, hurt, and blessing belongs. In his perfect timing, he will reveal how it all comes together.

Until then, keep your eyes on him, trust his process, and have faith that the final picture will be more beautiful than anything you could have imagined.

Reflect

- What "puzzle pieces" in your life don't seem to make sense?
- How can you trust God with the final picture?

Lord, life can be a bit puzzling at times. Help me to trust you with the pieces of my life and rely on you as my ultimate reference. In Jesus' name. Amen.

17

God's Masterpiece

For you created my inmost being; you knit me together in my mother's womb. I praise you because I am fearfully and wonderfully made; your works are wonderful, I know that full well.

PSALM 139:13–14 NIV

Have you ever been in awe of an artistic masterpiece? Standing before it and taking in all the intricate details while you think to yourself, *How on earth did someone manage to create such a beautiful thing?* Michelangelo's *David*, a tremendous marble sculpture, is a perfect depiction of artistic genius and human creativity.

With just a chisel and a hammer, Michelangelo chipped away at a massive slab of marble to reveal a masterpiece. He believed every block of stone had a statue inside of it and that it is the task of the sculptor to discover it. He could look at the material and envision the finished work before the true glory of it was ever revealed. When asked how he went about his sculpting process, he responded, "I saw the angel in the marble and carved until I set him free."[2]

---

2 Michelangelo, "Famous Quotes by Michelangelo," Michelangelo.org.

What if we took a moment to truly consider what God sees when he looks at us? Would we recognize that the slab of our lives is actually raw material for God to work with? Are we willing to surrender ourselves to him so that he may free us from the false ideas of self that we carry?

Just as Michelangelo carefully chipped away at a block of marble to reveal the masterpiece within, God, our divine Creator, continually shapes us. The Bible tells us that God is the potter, and we are the clay. He molds and refines our lives in his hands. The Potter's touch might feel firm, and the process might seem slow or uncomfortable, but every twist and turn of the wheel, every press of his hands, serves a purpose.

As clay, we must be pliable, allowing God to shape us according to his perfect will. Even when we feel imperfect, God does not discard us; instead, he reworks us into something new and beautiful. Before he knit us together in the wombs of our mothers, God saw all the intricate details of who we would become, and he knew exactly what he needed to do to get us there. He sees the potential within us just as a potter sees the potential in a lump of clay. In his skillful hands, our flaws are not final; they are simply parts of the process that lead to a greater purpose.

Still, when we allow the hand of God to break off all our unnecessary pieces, it can sometimes feel like a hammer to our pride and leave us completely unsure of what he's up to. Yet, if you have ever seen an artist at work, you will understand how difficult it is to visualize the end result when you're watching the process from the beginning. This is because art is created in stages, and the initial steps are all preparations that build on one another, leading up to the finished product.

We may sometimes find ourselves standing with our heads cocked sideways, wondering what on earth God is doing in our lives. When we're caught in the middle of his refining process, we may look at our lives and see nothing more than random chips and broken pieces, but that couldn't be further from reality. More likely than not, he is in the middle of preparing us to behold what he already sees in us. God will complete the masterpiece he started (Philippians 1:6).

Anything God chips away in us is done for the sole purposes of exposing something greater and making room for something new. When we allow our lives to be shaped by God, we eventually see that every experience adds layers and dimension to our lives. While we don't always understand what God is doing, we can trust that God is doing something good because we are his masterpiece, ready to be revealed one chip at a time.

Reflect

- What areas in your life do you believe God is sculpting and refining? How are you reacting to that sculpting process?
- Do you treat yourself like a masterpiece? Why or why not?
- Take a moment to reflect on how much thought and detail God put into creating you. Then identify three characteristics about yourself that you would like to thank him for.

Lord, thank you for creating me fearfully and wonderfully. Help me to see myself and others in the way that you see them. Help me to embrace the sculpting process and trust that you will reveal beautiful things to me in time. In Jesus' name. Amen.

18

Chats with a City Cowboy

I planted the seed, Apollos watered it,
but God has been making it grow.
1 CORINTHIANS 3:6 NIV

During my first year of college, I had a daily routine of taking the 6:30 a.m. city bus to school. It wasn't glamorous, but I grew to love the time it gave me in the morning to reflect, journal, and read. It also provided me with countless opportunities to see the most eclectic mix of people who got on and off the bus.

One rider stood out: a stout man with waist-length white hair who was wearing an all-black cowboy outfit and an expression as inviting as a slammed door. Yet somehow God brought us together—the grumpy old man with a chip on his shoulder and a chipper nineteen-year-old with a love for Jesus in her heart.

Our first conversation started during one of my usual morning rides. I sat leaning against the window, reading my Bible, when suddenly I heard a voice that sounded more like a growl. "I used to read that book but gave up on it a long time ago." I looked up to see the sullen cowboy in the seat across from me. Surprised he was speaking to me, I smiled and asked, "Why did you stop?" He hesitated before opening up about his past experiences and disbelief in God. This man needed someone to listen, and God used me to do just that.

As days turned to weeks, our bus-ride chats became a regular occurrence. He shared stories and his reasons for turning away from faith, and he never shied away from challenging my beliefs. He asked tough questions and tried to convince me that God does not exist, and then he would laugh at his inability to convince me. My city-cowboy friend didn't change his mind about God, but his hard demeanor softened—a sign that God was at work.

Then, one morning during our usual bus ride, he broke the news that he was moving and would no longer be taking the bus. We had one more heartfelt chat, and that was it. I never saw him again. For a long time after that, I felt discouraged not knowing what happened to him, like I failed because I hadn't successfully led him to Jesus. But God gently reminded me that the work he begins in someone's heart doesn't end when we're out of the picture.

If you've ever shared your faith and walked away without seeing results, you may have experienced similar feelings. We often think evangelism is a grand event where we have to lead someone to Christ in one conversation. In reality, evangelism is often an accumulation of seemingly insignificant moments where we show up, show love, and trust God with the outcome.

I have learned that any seed planted is a success in God's eyes. We may never see the full result of our efforts, but that does not mean our efforts are in vain or that we have failed. We don't need all the answers; what matters is our willingness to share, listen, and trust God to do the rest. Scripture reminds us of this truth: "My dear brothers and sisters, stand firm. Let nothing move you. Always give yourselves fully to the work of the Lord, because you know that your labor in the Lord is not in vain" (1 Corinthians 15:58).

Even when we don't see the immediate fruit of our labor, God is working in ways we will never fully understand. Our job is to plant the seeds, water them with prayer and love, and trust that God will bring the growth in his time. The seeds we plant today may take years to sprout, but God is faithful. Our efforts are never wasted in his hands.

As you reflect on this story, consider the seeds you've planted in the course of your own life. Who has God brought onto your path? Maybe there have been moments when you felt discouraged, wondering if you made any difference. Remember, evangelism isn't always about seeing results; it's about faithfulness in the small, everyday moments. It's trusting that God is always at work, bringing growth in his perfect timing.

Reflect

- How can you be more intentional in planting seeds of faith, even in small moments?
- Reflect on how God has worked through small moments in your life. How can you stay encouraged even without immediate results?

Lord, thank you for the opportunity to share your love. Help me trust your work in others' hearts, even when I can't see it. Give me courage, patience, and faithfulness. Use me as your vessel. In Jesus' name. Amen.

19

Nebuchad-Never Deny My God

They saw that the fire had not harmed their bodies, nor was a hair of their heads singed; their robes were not scorched, and there was no smell of fire on them.

DANIEL 3:27 NIV

We're in a world where values, political climates, and societal norms are constantly changing. While most can go along with ever-changing trends, we as Christians are called to walk a fine line of living in this world without allowing the world to live in us. But sometimes that fine line becomes a razor's edge, and we're pressured to conform to the world or face the consequences of standing for God. Shadrach, Meshach, and Abednego found themselves in exactly that situation—a moment where the pressure to conform wasn't just social; it was a matter of life and death.

Shadrach, Meshach, and Abednego, along with Daniel, were brought to serve King Nebuchadnezzar. The king built an enormous golden statue and commanded everyone to bow down and worship it. Failure to comply meant death. However, these young men of God stood their ground and refused to bow down. They said, "If we are thrown into the blazing furnace, the God we serve is able to deliver us from it, and he will deliver us from Your Majesty's hand" (Daniel 3:17).

Enraged, the king had the men thrown into the furnace. The heat was so intense that the soldiers who threw them into it were killed. While Shadrach, Meshach, and Abednego should have met the same fate, God had other plans. They were alive in the fire—"unbound," "unharmed," and with a fourth man who appeared like the "son of the gods" (Daniel 3:25). Astonished, King Nebuchadnezzar called them out. Not a hair on their heads was singed, and they did not smell of smoke. God met them in the flames and used their faithfulness to change the heart of a pagan king, leading Nebuchadnezzar to honor their God.

This miraculous story vividly depicts God's faithfulness and the power of standing firm when culture tells us to kneel down. The furnaces we face today may not involve literal flames, but they can feel just as intense.

Whether it's the pressure to conform in the workplace, the desire to fit in socially, or the exposure to media telling us to embrace worldly values, these challenges make it tempting to compromise our faith to avoid conflict. But as believers, we are called to live in this world but not be of it.

Unfortunately, many of us struggle to stand firm because modern versions of "bowing down" are far more subtle. Today, the pressure to conform often comes in the forms of staying silent when our faith is challenged in conversation, compromising our values to fit in at work or social gatherings, or allowing the media we consume to shape our beliefs and priorities. The pressure might be as simple as going along with the crowd to avoid conflict or accepting societal norms that contradict our faith—all in the name of progress.

These moments may not seem as dramatic as bowing before a statue, but they represent the same choice: Will we stand firm in our faith, or will we quietly conform to the world around us?

Truthfully, the answer can be complicated. Of course, as Christians, we want to honor God and be uncompromising in our faith, but how do we do that in a world inundated with laws, trends, lifestyles, and values that oppose God? Navigating this reality requires discernment. We ought to carefully consider when to take a stand and ask ourselves if the issue challenges the core of our faith and if it's an opportunity to witness by standing firm.

Not every situation demands confrontation, and sometimes the most powerful testimony is in living out our beliefs quietly yet steadfastly. However, when we do choose to stand, it's essential to do so with the purpose of honoring God, not demeaning others. In doing so, we reflect Christ's love and grace even in the midst of opposition.

Though the flames of scrutiny can tempt us to bend our morals in fear, it is our responsibility to stand firm in faith, knowing that God will protect us from the fiery trial. Remember that no weapon formed against us shall prosper (Isaiah 54:17).

As we face our furnaces, let us hold fast to the truth: the same God who delivered Shadrach, Meshach, and Abednego is with us today, ensuring we walk away unbound, unharmed, and unscorched by worldly flames.

Reflect

- Where do you feel pressured to conform?
- How can you rely on God in your "furnaces"?

Dear God, thank you for being with me in every trial. Help me to stand firm in my faith even when the pressure to conform feels overwhelming. Strengthen me, refine me, and use my faithfulness to reflect your glory. In Jesus' name. Amen.

20

Sheepish Beginnings

The LORD said to Samuel, "Do not consider his appearance or his height, for I have rejected him. The LORD does not look at the things people look at. People look at the outward appearance, but the LORD looks at the heart."

1 SAMUEL 16:7 NIV

For most of us, our daily lives have a familiar and somewhat mundane ebb and flow to them. A routine that isn't exactly dull nor too unusual. We go to work, run errands, manage our responsibilities. And at times, it can feel like we're just going through the motions. Living on autopilot, so to speak. That is, until something happens to break us out of our monotonous daze and become a catalyst for change.

Over the next three days, we'll be diving into the story of David and Goliath, a story that begins with a simple task and unfolds into a moment of divine destiny.

David's story begins as many of ours do: with a seemingly mundane routine. He was a young shepherd boy with a regular duty to care for the sheep and protect them from harm. Day after day, David faithfully carried out these responsibilities. Apart from the occasional battle with a lion or a bear threatening his flock, David's life was quite ordinary. But as we know, God has a way of taking the ordinary and using it for an extraordinary purpose.

On a day like any other, David's father, Jesse, sent him to run an errand delivering food to his older brothers who were fighting with the Israelite army. Little did David know that this trivial food delivery would set the stage for the miraculous deliverance of a divine nature—a moment that would change the course of his life and the fate of an entire nation.

The Israelites had been locked in conflict with the Philistines, one of their greatest and most persistent enemies. The Philistines were prepared for war and sent their greatest soldier to defeat them: Goliath, a Philistine giant. Goliath wasn't just tall; he was a behemoth, standing over nine feet tall with a presence that could send shivers down the spines of even the bravest soldiers.

For forty days, Goliath stood on the battlefield, challenging the Israelites to send out a warrior to fight him one-on-one. Each time he issued his challenge, the Israelites' response was the same: paralyzed fear.

When David arrived at the battlefield, he heard Goliath shouting his daily taunts at the Israelite army. Without hesitation, the boy with sheepish beginnings dared to question why Goliath hadn't met his end. David, a little shepherd boy, hadn't come to the battlefield to be a hero; he came to deliver lunch. Yet he somehow found himself there, not paralyzed by fear but moved by righteous indignation and a bold readiness to slay Goliath.

Most of us may already know the next part of the story, but let's take a moment to pause and reflect on David's "sheepish beginnings." David's journey reminds us that our lives, too, are filled with moments when the mundane can become miraculous.

We may think that what we're doing is insignificant, but God can use even the smallest actions to accomplish his greater purposes. The errands we run, the conversations we have, the small acts of obedience—all of these can be the very things that position us for something much greater than we could have imagined. The question is this: Will we be paralyzed with fear when God suddenly brings us there?

David's story challenges us to find comfort in the mundane but also to be ready and willing to embrace unexpected opportunities for change. It encourages us to recognize that our sheepish beginnings are not a limitation but a foundation that God can build upon. We don't have to be heroes in our own eyes; we just need to be faithful in the small things and trust that God knows how to bring us to the right place at the right time.

The tasks that seem trivial today could very well be setting the stage for miraculous deliverance in the days to come. Never underestimate the power of small beginnings because God doesn't. He sees the heart behind every action, and when the time is right, he will use your sheepish beginnings to do extraordinary things.

Reflect

- How has God used ordinary tasks in your life in extraordinary ways?
- What "Goliath" are you facing that may be causing you to feel paralyzed by fear? How can you find the courage to move in faith?

Abba, thank you for the reminder that even in the ordinary moments, you are working and preparing me for extraordinary things. Help me remain faithful with little and help me to trust that I am being prepared for so much more. When I face challenges that feel too difficult to overcome, help me to stand firm in faith as David did. In Jesus' name. Amen.

21

Nay to the Naysayers

David said to Saul, "Let no man's heart fail because of him. Your servant will go and fight with this Philistine."
1 Samuel 17:32 ESV

Let's pick back up with David's story. David had just arrived at the battlefield after his father had sent him on what seemed a regular errand of delivering lunch to David's brothers, but what David found was anything but regular. A giant named Goliath was taunting the armies of Israel, leaving them paralyzed with fear. Moved by righteous indignation, David asked nearby soldiers about Goliath and what would happen to the man who defeated him.

Eliab, David's eldest brother, overheard David asking questions and berated David for speaking up. Burning with anger, Eliab asked, "Why are you here? Who's watching those few sheep in the wilderness? I know your arrogance—you just came to watch the battle!" (1 Samuel 17:28 ESV). In modern terms, Eliab basically told David, "Go home, kid. Stick to your sheep. You're meddling in grown folks' business." To Eliab, David was meant for the fields, not the battlefield.

Ignoring his brother's doubt, David pressed on in questioning the soldiers. When King Saul heard about it, he summoned David, who boldly declared he would defeat Goliath. Like Eliab, Saul underestimated David: "You can't fight him; you're just a young man, and he's been a warrior since his youth" (1 Samuel 17:33 ESV). Saul couldn't see that David was more than just a youth; he was a child appointed by God.

Rather than being deterred by Saul's words, David was driven to challenge the giant. He spoke of his brawls with a lion and a bear in the fields and his plans to handle Goliath in the same manner. Compelled by David's persistence, Saul wished him well and placed a coat of armor upon him. "I cannot go in these," he said to Saul, "because I am not used to them" (1 Samuel 17:39 NIV). So, he removed the armor and fixed his mind for war.

This is a good stopping point to reflect on David's experience with Eliab. It is a perfect demonstration of the colloquial phrase "sometimes it be your own people." The first person to discourage David wasn't a stranger or an enemy; it was his own brother.

Eliab, who should have been supportive, instead chose to belittle and dismiss David. His experience shows us that, in our greatest times of need, the people closest to us sometimes offer the least support, which can be heartbreaking.

But, like David, when we place our security in the Lord above all else, we can fully embrace who God says we are instead of limiting ourselves to the version of ourselves people expect us to be.

Just as Saul placed his armor upon David, others will place their expectations upon us. Sometimes, intentionally or not, people try to mold us into the image that they think is best for us, but only we know what God has uniquely equipped us for. It's up to us to know when it is time to remove the weight of their opinions and move forward in God's truth.

When God calls us to a purpose, even those closest to us might not believe we're capable of fulfilling it. Instead of offering encouragement, they might dissuade us with doubts or project their fears onto us. This could look like a parent discouraging a dream they don't understand, a friend dismissing your passion, or a boss underestimating your abilities. We, like David, have to recognize that our true confidence comes from knowing who we are in Christ.

There will be times when others question or reject our ability because of what they see on the outside, but we are called to remember who we know: God Almighty. He equips us for the battles we are meant to fight, and he gives us the boldness to move forward, even when everything—or everyone—gives us reason to hold back. So, when others try to limit or define you, stand firm, knowing that God's calling on your life is stronger than any naysayer's doubt. You are equipped, you are chosen, and with God's strength, you can face any giant.

Reflect

- Recall a time when you felt discouraged by someone close to you. How did you respond?
- What "armor" or expectations have others tried to place on you that don't align with God's calling for your life? How can you shed them to follow God's purpose for you?

Oh, what a wonderful God you are, Lord. When I feel the weight of others' opinions, help me focus on yours. Fill me with radical boldness that surpasses expectation and teach me to stand firm in who you call me to be. In Jesus' name. Amen.

22

Slay That Giant

David said to the Philistine, "You come against me with sword and spear and javelin, but I come against you in the name of the Lord Almighty, the God of the armies of Israel, whom you have defied."

1 SAMUEL 17:45 NIV

From sheepish beginnings and lunch deliveries to Israel's army and frontline standoffs with giants, everything in David's life led him to this defining moment on the battlefield, the moment he would stand before Goliath. With nothing more than a few stones in a pouch, a sling in his hand, and a heart full of faith, David approached the Philistine giant.

Eyeing David and seeing he was little more than a boy, Goliath, with a heart of disdain, cursed David, saying, "Am I a dog, that you come at me with sticks?...Come here, and I'll give your flesh to the birds and the wild animals!" (vv. 43–44).

David looked up at the giant towering over him, and with an assurance that only God can provide, David declared that Goliath would meet his demise. He said to the Philistine,

> You come against me with sword and spear and javelin, but I come against you in the name of the Lord Almighty, the God of the armies of Israel, whom you have defied. This day the Lord will deliver you into my hands, and I'll strike you down and cut off your head. This very day I will give the carcasses of the Philistine army to the birds and the wild animals, and the whole world will know that there is a God in Israel.
>
> All those gathered here will know that it is not by sword or spear that the Lord saves; for the battle is the Lord's, and he will give all of you into our hands. (vv. 45–47)

Talk about a bold proclamation! Could you imagine being in David's position, facing a coldhearted, crusty colossus like Goliath? David was the least likely person to accomplish the task of killing a giant, but he refused to allow natural odds to overshadow the power of supernatural grace. David knew the God he served and was entirely prepared to serve Goliath a helping of truth and a whoopin' on the side.

Without faltering, David charged toward Goliath, whipped his shepherd's sling, and, with perfect aim, hurled a stone at the giant's forehead. The blaspheming enemy toppled to the ground. Then, as if to say, "Since you speak against my God like you've lost your whole mind, how about you lose your whole head too?" David unsheathed Goliath's sword and did just that. David slayed Goliath; the battle was won.

David's triumph over Goliath was more than winning a war; his story is an incredible reminder that, with God, we have the victory. But when our "giants" feel too big, giants of debt, sickness, anxiety, rejection, or depression, we sometimes find ourselves accepting defeat before we even step into the fight. The challenges loom over our heads, leaving us at a standstill, unsure if we even stand a chance. During times of doubt, we must remember that the same God who empowered David to defeat Goliath is with us today.

The battle belongs to the Lord, and with him by our side, no giant is too great to overcome. It's essential to hold onto the truth that God's power is made perfect in our weakness. When we face giants, it's not about our strength or capabilities but about our faith in the one who fights for us. Like David, we must trust that we are not fighting alone. We must trust that God will give us the courage and the means to confront and conquer whatever giants stand in our way.

So, whenever you feel overwhelmed by life's challenges, remember David's victory. No matter what giant you're facing—be it Goliath or something that feels just as formidable—trust that God is with you. His promises are bigger than any of our problems.

Step forward with the confidence that comes from knowing your battles are his to win, and he is always victorious. Take heart in the knowledge that God is your strength, your shield, and your deliverer. Trust in his power to slay every giant in your life, just as he did for David. With unwavering faith, let us march boldly forward, knowing that the Lord will deliver us from all our fears and enemies. The victory is already won; we only need to step out in faith and claim it.

Reflect

- What giants are you currently facing that feel too big to overcome?
- How can you trust God to help you conquer them?

Thank you, Jesus, for giving us victory over every enemy! Fill me with boldness to step forward in faith and trust that you will help me face every giant. Thanks to you, the battle is already won. In Jesus' name. Amen.

23

The Depths of Love

Judgment without mercy will be shown to anyone who has not been merciful. Mercy triumphs over judgment.

James 2:13 NIV

Let's dive into the story of Jonah and the whale (or big fish if we want to be technical). It's a Sunday school classic known to spark imagination, and it teaches valuable lessons about following God's instructions and asking for forgiveness after disobeying his commands. Though Jonah ran from God several times, his story emphasizes the fact that we can't outrun God. Today, however, we'll look at Jonah's story a little differently and focus on a different theme: loving our enemies.

God told the prophet Jonah to go to Nineveh, the capital of the Assyrian Empire, and preach against its sin. Sounds simple enough, right? Think again. Nineveh was no ordinary city; it was one of the most powerful and feared cities in the ancient world. It was known for its size, cultural achievements, wealth, and unparalleled brutality. Nineveh was not only powerful; it was notoriously wicked. The Assyrians invaded Israel, causing immense suffering and forced much of the population into exile.

As an Israelite, Jonah likely experienced the Assyrian's atrocities firsthand. The Ninevites embodied everything Jonah feared and hated, yet God wanted him to go to them and preach a message of mercy. Believing they deserved wrath, not mercy, Jonah fled in the opposite direction and boarded a ship to the farthest place he could think of.

After Jonah fled, God pursued him with a powerful storm, exposing his guilt to the sailors. Reluctantly, they cast him into the sea, where God, in compassion, sent a great fish to rescue him. For three days inside the fish, Jonah prayed and cried out to God. In the depths of the sea, Jonah encountered the depths of God's mercy—the same mercy he believed the Ninevites did not deserve, but God was still willing to offer it.

We should pause here and take an honest look at Jonah's reaction. He wasn't merely avoiding a difficult task; he was running from God's call to love in a way that felt impossible. Given his experiences, his response is not just understandable; it's relatable.

When faced with the command to love our enemies, everything in us wants to run the other way. We may find ourselves in the same boat as Jonah: committed to God but struggling with the pain of obedience when his call requires us to confront our deepest wounds. This is a dilemma we often find ourselves in when God calls us to love those who have wronged us.

When our hearts cry out for vengeance, but God calls us to show mercy, how do we respond? Are we really supposed to forget everything *they* said, all of the boundaries *they* crossed, every lie *they* told, and every hurt *they* caused? Is God really expecting us to just let *them* get away with wrongdoing while we suffer as a result? The answer is no: God does not expect us to ignore our pain or condone others' wrongful behavior. However, we are expected to forgive as we have been forgiven.

Forgiveness doesn't erase others' wrongs; it liberates us from the bitterness that can take root within us. The apostle Paul tells us to "see to it that no one fails to obtain the grace of God; that no 'root of bitterness' springs up and causes trouble, and by it many become defiled" (Hebrews 12:15 ESV). Perhaps a root of bitterness had sprung up in Jonah's heart, causing trouble and defiling his role as a prophet.

When left unchecked, a root of bitterness can grow so strong that it begins to break through the very foundation of our hearts, producing cracks in our relationships, our purposes, and our abilities to love as God intended.

When we find ourselves running away from God's call, tossing in a sea of bitterness, or feeling like we've gone emotionally overboard, let's remember that God is with us in the depths. Beneath the weight of it all, God will provide us with a space to cry out to him—a place where we can confront the contents of our hearts and be transformed by a love that is deeper than our bitterness.

Reflect

- Who are the "Ninevites" in your life—those you find hardest to forgive or show mercy to?
- How can you begin to release the bitterness in your heart and allow God's love to transform you?

Lord, help me to forgive as you have forgiven me. Remove any bitterness in my heart and fill me with your love, even for those who have hurt me. Transform my heart with your mercy. In Jesus' name. Amen.

24

Delilah de Liah

Guard your heart above all else,
for it determines the course of your life.
PROVERBS 4:23 NLT

There is something so refreshing about a good love story: boy meets girl, sparks fly, they fall in love, and live happily ever after—the end. Or, a less refreshing tale: boy meets girl, sparks fly, girl lies and then betrays boy by cutting off the source of his strength, a.k.a. his flowing locks. Sound familiar?

The story of Samson and Delilah is one that leaves many believers scratching their heads, or at the very least, running their fingers through their hair. How could a man so strong be so easily deceived?

Samson was no ordinary man. He was chosen by God, blessed with incredible strength, and set apart as a Nazarite from birth. His Nazarite vow, which included abstaining from wine, avoiding contact with the dead, and never cutting his hair, marked him as consecrated to God. As a judge of Israel, Samson held significant spiritual and political authority, and his people revered him for his strength and his role in God's plan to deliver the Israelites from Philistine oppression. Yet, his unparalleled strength led to a significant weakness: he let his guard down around the wrong person.

Delilah—a cunning, charming, and persistent Philistine woman—proved to be a dangerous companion. The Philistine rulers, desperate to neutralize the threat that Samson posed, offered Delilah a substantial sum to uncover the secret of his strength. Recognizing an opportunity, she eagerly obliged.

Relentlessly, Delilah wielded her charm as a weapon, feigning weakness and masking her intentions under the guise of innocent curiosity—a tactic reminiscent of the serpent's deception of Eve in the garden of Eden. Samson, blinded by his own security, failed to see the danger. Believing she could be trusted, he eventually revealed that his hair was the source of his power. Armed with this knowledge, Delilah lulled him to sleep and let the Philistines cut his hair. With the source of his strength now severed, Samson broke his Nazarite vow.

The story of Samson's downfall is more than a tale about strong, silky strands and sneaky buzzcuts. It's a stark reminder of how the Enemy will use the wrong people at the right time to derail our calling. Many of us have sadly experienced the pain of betrayal—a wound that cuts deep and, with the twist of a blade, leaves us feeling weak and vulnerable long after trust has been severed.

At the risk of being vulnerable myself, I know the pain of betrayal all too well. I am a survivor of emotional and psychological abuse, and I understand the scars of shame that betrayal can leave behind. Like Samson, who after losing his strength was captured by the Philistines and made into a spectacle, we may feel humiliated by our failures to recognize deception.

Betrayal doesn't discriminate. The Enemy often uses those closest to us—family members, friends, colleagues, or even spiritual leaders—to inflict the deepest wounds, leading us to doubt our own judgment, our worth, and the goodness in others. But here's the critical lesson: though Samson's physical strength was taken from him, his story didn't end in defeat.

In his darkest hour, blind and bound in a Philistine temple, Samson turned to God. He prayed for strength one last time, and God, in his mercy, granted it. With his final act, Samson brought down the temple, destroying his enemies.

Now, let me be clear—this does not mean we should say a prayer and start bopping our enemies upside the head (tempting as that may be). This means that no matter how deeply we have been deceived or how weak we have been made to feel, God is the source of our strength.

When we vow to honor God, it does not matter what the enemies in our lives do to harm us; God will heal our wounds and vindicate us. He takes what the

Enemy meant for evil and turns it for our good. We may stumble and fall, we may be bruised and battered by life's battles, but God's grace is always sufficient to lift us back up. Samson's story is a testament to the fact that our failures and weaknesses do not have the final say—God does.

Reflect

- Are there relationships in your life in which you've let your guard down? How might you seek God's wisdom in guarding your heart better?
- How can you turn to God for strength and healing in moments when betrayal has left you feeling vulnerable and weak?

Lord, help me to discern the "Delilahs" in my life and guard my heart with your wisdom. When I am weak, remind me that you are my strength. Heal my wounds and turn my pain into purpose. In Jesus' name. Amen.

25

Cocka-Doodle-Doom

The Lord turned and looked at Peter. Then Peter remembered the word of the Lord, how He had said to him, "Before the rooster crows, you will deny Me three times."

LUKE 22:61 NKJV

Have you ever heard the expression "Never say never"? It is typically used in response to a definitive statement like "I'll never get married," "I'll never run a marathon," or "I'll never eat that much pizza again." While remarks like these may be spoken with conviction, they often fail to come to fruition.

"Never say never" reminds us that life is unpredictable, and what seems certain today might not hold true tomorrow. One of the most memorable "Never say never" moments took place on the night of the Last Supper. In the dim light of the evening, Jesus and his twelve disciples reclined at a table to enjoy a Passover meal.

After demonstrating the first communion and telling them that someone at the table would betray him, Jesus and the Twelve made their way to the Mount of Olives. Once there, Jesus looked to them and said, "Tonight all of you will fall away because of me" (Matthew 26:31 CSB). In response, Peter boldly proclaimed that he would never deny Jesus, even if it meant he would die. But Peter quickly learned that, just as Jesus warned, he would not only deny him but do so three times before the rooster crowed.

As the events of Jesus' betrayal escalated and the disciples fled, Peter had three opportunities to publicly profess Jesus: the first when a servant woman recognized him as a disciple, but he denied it; the second when another noticed him, but Peter claimed he was not one of the twelve; and the third when another identified him as a Galilean with Jesus, but Peter acted as if he had no idea what the man meant.

While Peter was still speaking and denying his connection to Jesus, the rooster crowed. The Lord then looked at Peter, who remembered what Jesus had said: "Before the rooster crows you will deny Me three times." Peter wept bitterly. He had every intention of honoring God with his commitment and was devastated to have failed Jesus.

It is easy to judge Peter for his denial, but how often do we do the same? How often have we been certain of our own strength only to find ourselves quickly discovering the extent of our weakness? We boldly profess our loyalty and devotion, but in moments of fear, pressure, or temptation, we find ourselves falling short.

It reminds me of the apostle Paul's words in Romans 7:15: "I do not understand what I do. For what I want to do I do not do, but what I hate I do" (NIV). This verse relates to the inner conflict we experience as believers. Our hearts may deeply desire to love God perfectly, but because we fall short of his glory, we can only love him to the best of our human ability. This is something that Jesus so graciously reminded Peter of after his resurrection.

As recorded in John 21:15–17, Jesus asked Peter three times—drawing a parallel to his three denials—if Peter loved him. These three questions placed an emphasis on Peter's need to unwaveringly commit to the Lord in the future, but they also held a deeper significance.

When Jesus asked Peter, "Do you love me?" he used the Greek word *agape*, which refers to unconditional love. Peter responded with the Greek word *phileo*, which refers more to a brotherly type of love. Peter was aware that his love for God was not unconditional but rather natural and came with limitations. *Agape* love, on the other hand, is a divine level of love that only God can have. Yet, through Christ and the indwelling Holy Spirit, we can share *agape* love with others.

When we fail to love God or others in an *agape* way, it should not be seen as grounds for condemnation but rather an invitation to let God continuously perfect us in love and teach us what love is not.

As you meditate on this story, I urge you to read 1 Corinthians 13:4–8. Meditate on this definition of *agape* love. Then prayerfully consider where the metaphorical roosters may be crowing in your life. Reflect on areas in your heart where God may be asking, "Do you *agape* love me?" Then, rest in knowing that God, who loves you unconditionally, will continue to teach you how to *agape* love.

Reflect

- How can you grow in *agape* love?
- Read 1 Corinthians 13:4–8 and replace the word *love* with your name. What came to mind when doing this?

Lord, thank you for your agape love. Help me to love in this way and to stand firm in that love toward you. In Jesus' name. Amen.

26

Burning with Doubt

Moses said to God, "Who am I that I should go to Pharaoh and bring the Israelites out of Egypt?"
Exodus 3:11 NIV

In Exodus 3, we learn that Moses, arguably one of the greatest prophets of the Old Testament, was tending the flock of his father-in-law, Jethro, and took them to Mount Horeb. When he arrived, Moses noticed a bush that was consumed by fire but not burning up.

When Moses approached the burning bush, God called out to him and proclaimed, "Do not come any closer. Take off your sandals, for the place where you are standing is holy ground" (Exodus 3:5). Could you imagine being in the sandals of Moses in this scenario? Truly, if I were minding my business on a mountaintop and God Almighty chose to speak to me through a burning bush, I would probably think I lost my mind and would run away in fear.

The Bible explains that Moses, too, felt fear in this moment: "Moses hid his face, because he was afraid to look at God" (v. 6). As God spoke, he told Moses to go to Pharaoh and bring the Israelites out of Egypt. In response to God's mighty call, Moses expressed four concerns and made one request.

1. Who am I to go to Pharaoh? (v. 11)
2. What if they ask me your name? (v. 13)
3. What if they don't believe me? (Exodus 4:1)
4. I am not eloquent. (v. 10)
5. Please send someone else. (v. 13)

Over the next five days, we will journey with Moses as he wrestled with doubt and insecurity in response to God's call. We will explore each of Moses' concerns, reflecting on how they mirror our own struggles with self-doubt and how God's reassurances speak directly to our hearts.

Moses' first question to God ("Who am I to go to Pharaoh?") is likely similar to the questions we ask ourselves when confronted with feelings of inadequacy and self-doubt, especially when we are confronted with a call or task that is far outside our comfort zone. (Full transparency, the process of writing my first book has definitely given me plenty of "Who am I?" moments.)

When God called to Moses through the burning bush and told him to go to Pharaoh in Egypt, the thought of doing so must have been a lot for Moses to process. Prior to this mountaintop moment with God, Moses had killed an Egyptian while protecting a fellow Hebrew and fled from Egypt to the land of

Midian, where he had lived for forty years. It had presumably been decades since Moses had been to Egypt, but God chose him to be the one to deliver the Israelites from Pharaoh. And when Moses asked the question, "Who am I to go to Pharaoh?" it revealed his underlying feeling of inadequacy.

We may not be called by God to oppose a pharaoh, but we are called by God to do *something*. What is that something for you? Have you felt feelings of inadequacy rise up within you? If that is the case, you are not alone. Wrestling with doubt and experiencing feelings of inadequacy is a common part of the human experience.

The great news is we do not have to wrestle with those doubts and feelings alone. Like Moses, we can be transparent with God in prayer, and we can express our concerns openly to him. 1 Peter 5:7 tells us to "cast all [our] anxiety on him because he cares for [us]."

God responded to Moses' fear with compassion and reassurance when he said, "I will be with you" (Exodus 3:12). Take a moment to imagine the Lord responding to your doubts in the same loving way.

God's presence and support are what empowers us to overcome doubt and fulfill his calling for us. So, during times when we question who we are, let's remind ourselves that "the one who calls you is faithful, and he will do it" (1 Thessalonians 5:24). That is without question.

Reflect

- What doubts or insecurities can you surrender to God today?
- Meditate on these words of God: "I am with you." How does this make you feel?

Lord, in moments of doubt, please help me to focus on your ability more than my inability. Empower me to do what you have called me to do, regardless of how I feel. In Jesus' name. Amen.

27

Name It and Claim It

Moses said to God, "If I come to the people of Israel and say to them, 'The God of your fathers has sent me to you,' and they ask me, 'What is his name?' what shall I say to them?" God said to Moses, "I Am Who I Am."

Exodus 3:13–14 ESV

In yesterday's devotion, we reflected on Moses' initial response to God's call, specifically Moses' doubt and feelings of inadequacy. Today, we will look into Moses' second question: "What should I say to them if they ask me your name?" This question, similar to his first, is rooted in doubt but also sprinkled with a dash of people-pleasing.

Imagine you're Moses for a moment. You've been tasked with the daunting responsibility of delivering the Israelites from oppression and leading them out of Egypt. Not only is God asking you to go back to the place you ran away from but also to convince an entire nation that you're not *One Flew Over the Cuckoo's Nest* crazy.

Many of us would feel the need to gain the Israelites' trust and convince them to believe us, which could become a burden and fill our hearts with doubt.

Moses seemed to experience this as well. He wanted to approach the Israelites with an authority greater than his own, which is why he asked God to reveal his name so that Moses could establish credibility among the people.

God heard Moses' request and responded: "I Am Who I Am" In Hebrew, *ehyeh asher ehyeh* translates to "I will be what I will be." By using this name, God was assuring Moses and the Israelites that he was everything they needed him to be. It declared his sufficiency, reliability, and power. Yet, like many of us today, Moses struggled with the fear that others would judge or reject him. His concern showcases our natural desire to be accepted and validated by our peers.

How often do we, like Moses, wonder what other people will think of us and our decisions? While a select few have truly mastered the art of "who gives a dang" when it comes to the opinions of others, some of us may not find that so easy to do. From splurging on the latest trendy shoes because we want to look cool to piling more work onto our plates that we don't have capacity for (because we don't want to let anyone down by saying no), it can be easy to blur the lines between considering others and striving to please them.

As a recovering people-pleaser myself, I know firsthand how difficult it can be to break out of that mindset and the habits that come with it. We all want to feel like we belong, and we all want to be well-received, but if we put too much weight into the opinions of others, it can destroy our confidence and perpetuate even more anxiety. And if we prioritize the approval of others above our own, we risk jeopardizing our values, our convictions, or even our call from God.

In Galatians 1:10 we read from the apostle Paul, "Am I now seeking the approval of man, or of God? Or am I trying to please man? If I were still trying to please man, I would not be a servant of Christ." Paul makes it unmistakably clear that we must choose: either seek the eternal approval of God or chase the fleeting approval of man.

God's response, "I Am Who I Am," serves as a powerful reminder that our validation comes from God, not people. When we stand on the mighty name of Jesus and depend on his inconceivable might, we find the courage to move forward in faith despite any fears of what other people might think.

As we continue to meditate on Moses' questions and God's responses, let's reflect on our own lives and remind ourselves where our true validation comes from. Let's respond to the call of God with confidence, knowing that no matter what people think, it is the opinions of "I Am" that matter most.

Reflect

- What does the name "I Am Who I Am" tell you about the nature and character of God?
- In what areas of your life do you find yourself seeking approval from others? How does this affect your behavior?

Lord, sometimes I feel pressure to please others, or I put too much value on their opinions of me. Help me to remember that my validation is found in you. In Jesus' name. Amen.

28

Is Dis Belief?

Moses answered, "What if they do not believe me or listen to me and say, 'The Lord did not appear to you'?"

Exodus 4:1 NIV

So far, we have taken a deeper look at Moses' initial feelings of inadequacy and his desire to gain credibility with the Israelites by sharing the mighty name of God. We also addressed the truth that "I Am Who I Am" is with us, and our validation is found in him.

Today we will address Moses' third question: "What if they do not believe me or listen to me and say, 'The Lord did not appear to you'?" (Exodus 4:1). This question highlights the fear of rejection or dismissal from others, which is something many of us experience in our personal, professional, and spiritual lives.

Moses was concerned about the optics of his situation. Let's put ourselves in his sandals again and really ask ourselves how we would react in his position. Imagine that today, right now, God presented himself to you through a burning house plant and told you to travel to a distant land where he would use you to deliver an entire nation from oppression.

I don't want to speak for all of you, but I know *I* would most certainly have questions. How am I getting there? Is my airfare divinely covered? The people won't have any clue who I am; what do I tell them? How do I explain myself when I get there? What if they laugh in my face? Will they think I'm crazy when I tell them God spoke to me through a flaming hydrangea?

It is sometimes too easy for us to forget that people in the Bible were just as flawed as we are. Moses' fear of being rejected or dismissed was rooted in a genuine concern about whether or not the people would take him seriously.

God responded to Moses by guiding him in performing three miraculous acts, and he told Moses to perform them again before the Israelites. These acts would serve as signs that Moses was indeed acting on God's behalf. Let's explore each sign and its significance.

1. God turns Moses' staff into a snake.

In Exodus 4:2–4, God asked Moses what he was holding in his hand. After Moses said it was a staff, God instructed him to throw it to the ground. The staff turned into a snake, and when Moses grabbed it by the tail, it turned back into a staff again.

This sign reminds us that God can use whatever we give him. He may be calling you to do something that stirs up a lot of fear. Before you allow that fear to run rampant or allow doubt to dominate your thoughts, remember this: God literally used a stick. Why wouldn't he use you?

2. God turns Moses' hand leprous and heals it.

God instructed Moses to put his hand into his cloak, and when Moses took it out, it was leprous—white as snow. Then God told Moses to put his hand back into the cloak and remove it again, and his hand was restored (Exodus 4:6–7).

In biblical times, leprosy was considered a serious and incurable disease. Something in your life might seem incurable or hopeless, but the message we can pull from this second sign is that God has the power to heal and restore—no matter how bad things might look.

3. God promises to turn water into blood.

God told Moses that if the people did not believe the first and second signs, then Moses was to pour water from the Nile onto dry ground, and the water would turn into blood (Exodus 4:8–9).

Unbeknownst to Moses, this sign foreshadowed the plague that later occurred when the entire Nile River turned into blood. God already knew all that would pass, including the Israelites believing and following Moses.

If you ever find yourself fearing the future or worrying if people will take your call seriously, keep in mind that if God calls you to it, he'll give you everything you need to do it.

We serve a God who empathizes with our weaknesses and equips us in every way. He is patient with us in times of doubt, and he comforts us when we're overcome with fear. Remember that the same God who was with Moses is also with you. And that, my friend, is a sure sign of acceptance.

Reflect

- How does Moses' story resonate with your own feelings of fear and doubt?
- What signs have you experienced in your life that remind you that God is with you?

Lord, thank you for every sign you have placed in my life and for comforting me in times of fear. Help me not to be led by fear but to rest in the assurance that I am loved and accepted by you. In Jesus' name. Amen.

29

Dangerously Misunderstood

"Pardon your servant, Lord. I have never been eloquent, neither in the past nor since you have spoken to your servant. I am slow of speech and tongue."
EXODUS 4:10 NIV

As we have taken a closer look at the story of the burning bush, we have watched Moses wrestle with self-doubt, feelings of inadequacy, questions about his own worth, and fear of rejection. Despite God's constant reassurances and miraculous signs, Moses remained hesitant.

"Pardon your servant, Lord. I have never been eloquent, neither in the past nor since you have spoken to your servant. I am slow of speech and tongue." In other words, Moses did not believe he was a good public speaker, and he doubted he would be effective with the people because of this perceived flaw.

Moses' fear of public speaking also speaks to a broader fear of being misunderstood. Whether consciously or not, most of us are aware that the presence of conflict is often found in the absence of understanding. That's why many of us feel threatened by the possibility of being misunderstood.

We may have the best intentions, but if those intentions aren't communicated clearly or our actions are misinterpreted, we risk social, economic, or relational strain. So, too, was Moses aware of the tension that could arise if he failed to communicate effectively with Pharoah and the Israelites.

God had already assured Moses three times that God would be with him and use him to deliver the Israelites, so when Moses responded to God's assurances with yet another objection, it became clear that Moses' reluctance went beyond fear and doubt. It was an excuse that showed a deeper unwillingness to obey God's calling.

In Exodus 4:11–12, the Lord said to Moses, "Who gave human beings their mouths? Who makes them deaf or mute? Who gives them sight or makes them blind? Is it not I, the Lord? Now go; I will help you speak and will teach you what to say."

Anyone who has been corrected or disciplined by a caregiver or teacher may recognize what's really happening here between God and Moses. When I was growing up, for example, every now and then my mom would reply to my teenage sass with a stern "Who do you think you're talking to?" God was firmly but lovingly correcting Moses by reminding him of his authority. Sometimes, we, too, need a firm reminder of who God is in our lives.

When we're afraid of being misunderstood, it is essential for us to remember that God brings understanding; in fact, his understanding has no limit (Psalm 147:5). If we are willing to cling to he who understands, we can overcome the fear of being misunderstood. Whether we're unsure of how to share our faith with someone, or what to say in a difficult or uncomfortable situation, or how to get our message across to others, God will guide us through it.

Even though Moses doubted the power of his voice, God still spoke through him to warn Pharaoh and to lead the Israelites out of Egypt. This shows us that sometimes, the parts of us that seem the least useful or helpful are the very parts that God intends to use the most. The same God who made our mouths will give us words to speak. The same God who formed our eyes will help us see what needs to be seen. The same God who created us knows exactly how to use us.

Today, let's take a step of faith and move beyond our fears. Let's devote time to reflect on who God is in our lives and all that he has done in his power and authority. Instead of depending on our own ability to convey a point, let us keep God's sovereignty and assurances in mind. Our Lord is mighty in power, and he is able to do exceedingly more than we can do ourselves.

Reflect

- How might you be leaning on your own understanding right now?
- How can you trust God's guidance more willingly?

Lord, thank you for the clarity and understanding you bring. Give me the courage to do what you have called me to do and the words to say when I fear being misunderstood. In Jesus' name. Amen.

30

Not My Job

"Now go! I will be with you as you speak, and I will instruct you in what to say." But Moses again pleaded, "Lord, please! Send anyone else."

Exodus 4:12–13 NLT

For the past four days, we have examined the concerns that Moses expressed to God at the burning bush. Each of Moses' doubts revealed deep-seated insecurities and a reluctance to perform the tasks God set before him. Today, we'll focus on Moses' final statement: "Lord, please! Send anyone else."

God became angry with Moses. After all, Moses was letting his doubts take precedence over God's truth. This was not the anger of a fragile and unjust ruler but rather the righteous frustration of a loving father watching insecurity and fear consume his child.

Though angry, God continued to show Moses compassion and suggested that Moses' brother, Aaron, go with him. In Exodus 4:16, God says to Moses, "Aaron will be your spokesman to the people. He will be your mouthpiece, and you will stand in the place of God for him, telling him what to say."

Here's the thing. God providing Moses with Aaron as a spokesman was incredibly gracious, but it begs the question: Was Aaron truly necessary to fulfill God's call? The purpose behind this question is not meant to undermine the significance of Aaron's role in delivering the Israelites but to prompt us to consider why God actually sent him.

God had already assured Moses that he would be with him. He empowered Moses to perform miraculous signs to demonstrate God's power, and he declared exactly what Moses was supposed to do and why. So certainly, whether Aaron was there or not, God was going to use Moses to deliver the Israelites out of Egypt.

Still, God accommodated Moses' insecurity by sending Aaron with him. This leads me to believe that Aaron was not sent for the call but for the confidence. Moses lacked the confidence that he was someone who could be used by God. This lack of confidence is hardly exclusive to Moses though.

We all face daunting situations at some point. Whether it's God calling us to confront our fears, heal from insecurity, or step out in a way that we haven't before, we might suddenly become painstakingly aware of our inadequacies and want to plead with God to assign the task to someone else. Instead of trusting God to equip us and fill in the gaps, we look for the

"Aarons" in our lives. Our lack of confidence becomes a barrier to our obedience.

Instead of wondering if we are enough, we should ask ourselves if we believe God is enough. Will we trust him to do what we can't, or will we throw in the towel when we feel useless?

We do not have to conquer every fear and rid ourselves of every doubt. We just have to be willing to follow God despite those fears and doubts. We have to embrace the process of becoming all that God wants us to become and remember that God does extraordinary things with ordinary people.

In Exodus 3 and 4, Moses is insecure. But by Numbers 12, God describes Moses as humble—the most humble man on the earth, in fact (v. 3). Though Moses did have many flaws, one of his great strengths was his ability and willingness to openly express himself to God. Some of us may scoff at Moses questioning God, but we should learn from him.

When we bring our doubts, fears, and hang-ups to the feet of Jesus, he is faithful to offer us assurance and proper perspective. He will correct our skewed concept of self, challenge our dependence on others, remind us where our authority comes from, and help us in our unbelief. He will faithfully provide us with everything and everyone we need to grow into the person he has called us to be.

Let us posture our hearts in the same way. Let's take off our sandals of self-doubt and kneel before our almighty God, acknowledging our shortcomings while depending on his miraculous strength.

Reflect

- In what ways have you looked for an "Aaron" to support you rather than fully trusting in God's promise to be with you?
- How can you shift your focus to rely more on God's strength?

Lord, I surrender to you and ask that you would help me remember how mighty you are. Increase my ability to depend on you and not seek refuge in others. In Jesus' name. Amen.

31

Baby Steps

The Lord makes firm the steps of the one who delights in him; though he may stumble, he will not fall, for the Lord upholds him with his hand.

Psalm 37:23–24 NIV

My nephew Harley took his first steps when he was about ten months old. My heart filled with joy as I watched him stagger toward my sister like a pot-bellied pirate. We all cheered in celebration with every step. He had just hit a major milestone, and we were beyond thrilled.

Though Harley continued to stumble and fall, eventually, his legs strengthened—so much so that today, he has nearly turned into a little ninja warrior. This reminds me of a Bible passage: "For though the righteous fall seven times, they rise again" (Proverbs 24:16).

Every believer is at a different stage in their walk with God. Some may be learning to stand, some beginning to walk, and others might be running in the things of God with zeal. Yet, no matter how new or mature our walk with God is, all of us occasionally stumble. Even though our goal is to avoid falling altogether, sometimes we lose our footing.

Consider this story about Peter, a disciple who confidently stepped out of a boat to walk on water toward Jesus. In Matthew 28–31, Peter said, "Lord, if it is You, command me to come to You on the water." Jesus invited him, and Peter began walking closer. But when he saw the wind and waves, fear took hold, and he began to sink, crying out, "Lord, save me!" Immediately, Jesus reached out his hand and caught him, saying, "You of little faith, why did you doubt?" (v. 31 NASB).

Peter's experience offers a vivid illustration of our spiritual journey. He had moments of strong faith and moments of doubt, during which he stumbled. But each time Peter faltered, Jesus was there, extending a hand to lift him up. He does the same with us, extending grace toward us whenever we inevitably fall. He God does not condemn us but encourages us to continue our journey. We must trust his helping hand because, when we do lose our footing, we need him to help us get back up again.

Think of David, who Scripture describes as a man after God's own heart (1 Samuel 13:14). He experienced many, many falls in his life. He grievously sinned with Bathsheba. He committed adultery and then tried to cover it up with deceit and murder. Despite these serious failures, when David was confronted by the prophet Nathan, he immediately repented.

In Psalm 51, we find a heartfelt prayer of repentance, in which David asked God to create in him a clean heart and renew a steadfast spirit within him. David's story shows us that even when we fall, sincere repentance and a turn back to God allow us to continue our journey.

Just as a baby learning to walk finds encouragement at each step, God rejoices over every inch we move toward him. Our desire should be to walk uprightly in holiness, but God understands our human frailty. Psalm 103:13–14 says, "As a father has compassion on his children, so the Lord has compassion on those who fear him; for he knows how we are formed, he remembers that we are dust."

The devil will try to keep us down after we've fallen. He'll whisper lies that we have done too much wrong to turn back to God. Yet we have to cultivate our ability to tune out his lies and fix our eyes back on Jesus. Because of the Lord's sacrifice, we can come boldly before God no matter how many times we fall. We can approach his throne of grace with confidence and receive all that we need to press on (Hebrews 4:16).

God, after all, is not standing over us with disappointment. He is cheering us on like a loving parent, delighted with our every attempt to walk closer to him. He looks beyond our shaky strides to see the hearts of the people who take them. He will secure your steps and help you through your pot-bellied-pirate moments. Every step toward God is a step closer to maturing into the person you were created to be. And that is always worth celebrating.

Reflect

- Think about a recent time when you stumbled. How did you respond?
- David repented sincerely after his fall. Are there areas in your life where you need to seek God's forgiveness?

Lord, thank you for picking me up whenever I fall. Thank you, too, that as I run this race, you cheer me on every step of the way. Help me to walk confidently toward you. In Jesus' name. Amen.

32

Having a Martha Moment

"Be still, and know that I am God. I will be exalted among the nations, I will be exalted in the earth!"

Psalm 46:10 esv

Between work deadlines, school drop-offs, household chores, ministry duties, and relationship maintenance, a lot of us are just too busy to be still. When we have so much on our plates, it can be challenging to shift from a state of business to a place of rest. We see this struggle particularly within the church.

Many of us have grown so accustomed to serving that we unknowingly act more like busybodies than blissful brides of Christ. Our service is good, of course, but the story of Martha and Mary reminds us that sitting in the presence of Jesus is far better.

In Luke 10:38–42, Jesus and his disciples visited a village after a woman named Martha had invited them into her home. As Martha served the men, her sister Mary sat at the feet of Jesus to listen to his teachings.

Now, before we continue delving into the biblical text, let's take a moment to consider how we would react in this situation. Imagine that a president or prime minister of your choice and a few of their friends are coming to your house for dinner.

You probably wouldn't serve your run-of-the-mill instant-noodles to such prominent people. No, you would see this experience as an honor and privilege, an opportunity that would inspire you to whip out your best recipes, finest china, and most hospitable manners. It would be a lot of work requiring a tremendous amount of help. How would you feel if your so-called help was doing everything but helping? I'm willing to guess that, like Martha, many of us would feel frustrated and annoyed.

When Martha saw her sister sitting instead of helping, I envision her standing with a pop in her hip, some sort of biblical cooking utensil in hand, and an expression that would send most running for the hills. She said, "Lord, do you not care that my sister has left me to serve alone? Tell her then to help me" (v. 40).

Have you ever been in a situation where you felt like you were the only one carrying the weight of responsibility? You were working incredibly hard, but everyone else—and maybe their mommas, too, were taking a break? It can be incredibly disheartening and, in some cases, lead us to feel wronged and entitled to their support.

While there are certainly cases when others choose to be lazy, is it also possible that we're simply doing more than what's necessary? Is it that we're unable to take a break or unwilling to slow down? Jesus' response to Martha highlights an important point. He turned to her and said, "Martha, Martha, you are anxious and troubled about many things, but one thing is necessary. Mary has chosen the good portion, which will not be taken away from her" (vv. 41–42).

Jesus essentially told Martha that she was concerned about everything but the most important thing, which was being present with the Lord. From Martha's perspective, her service showed her devotion and love for God. But from Jesus' perspective, Mary's stillness showed her desire for closeness and intimacy with God.

When we're caught having a Martha moment, our minds may be overwhelmed with all of our obligations, responsibilities, and to-do's. This leaves little to no room for rest. God honors our service to him, but we must prioritize *being* with him. This is not to imply that our labor is in vain, but it does point out that our labor should not take precedence over a deep relationship with God.

So, when our plates are still full, how do we find balance between the sometimes-unavoidable Martha moments and the time we want to sit at the feet of Jesus? Like most meaningful relationships, we have to be intentional about it.

Just as we make the time to do all that we need to do in our lives, we must also make the time to be all that we are with God. To sit at his feet, meditate on his teachings, and know that he is a God worthy of our stillness. As we go about our busy lives, let's make it a priority to do just that.

Reflect

- Reflect on times when you have been overly busy with life. How has this impacted your relationship with God?
- How can you be intentional about making time to simply be with Jesus?

Lord, thank you that I can sit at your feet. Help me not to be so busy that I neglect my time with you. May I prioritize being in your presence. In Jesus' name. Amen.

33

A Foreign Affair

"No one can serve two masters, since either he will hate one and love the other, or he will be devoted to one and despise the other. You cannot serve both God and money."

MATTHEW 6:24 CSB

I recently heard a story of a beachgoer who accidentally drifted out to sea on a…flamingo floatie. Thirty-six hours later, rescuers spotted the pink PVC flamingo floating in open water fifty miles away from shore. Thankfully, the stranded woman was successfully rescued.

I can only imagine the look on her face when she opened her eyes, expecting to see the beach but finding herself lost at sea. Talk about a wake-up call! Like our flamingo-floating friend, we may unknowingly drift in a spiritual sense—not because we set out to but because comfort and routine can lull us into complacency. We lose sight of God's plan and get swept away by our own.

Slowly, little by little, we drift until we realize one day how far we've strayed. King Solomon, the wisest and richest man in the Bible, is a perfect example of what can happen when we take our eyes off God.

At the beginning of his reign, Solomon ruled faithfully, built the temple, and led the nation in worship. However, despite Solomon's unmatched wisdom, he still made foolish decisions when it came to relationships. He was a ladies' man, a flirtatious fellow, a bit of a biblical bachelor if you will. According to 1 Kings 11:3, Solomon had seven hundred wives of royal birth and three hundred concubines, totaling one thousand women.

In Deuteronomy 7:3–4, God commands Israel: "You shall not intermarry with them, giving your daughters to their sons or taking their daughters for your sons, for they would turn away your sons from following me, to serve other gods. Then the anger of the LORD would be kindled against you, and he would destroy you quickly" (ESV).

Instead of listening to God's clear instruction, Solomon let his love for beauty override his godly duty. He blatantly went against God's instruction and seemed to put a ring on darn near every foreign woman's finger. Unsurprisingly, just as God warned, Solomon's wives influenced him, and he began to worship their false gods. He built high places and altars for idols and, as some may say, got "lost in the sauce." He completely lost touch with reality, and in his own arrogance, he behaved in a manner that was detestable to the Lord.

Because of Solomon's choices, God ultimately decided it was time to revoke his privileges. His descendants would no longer inherit the kingdom they were once destined to receive, and his reign, which began with such blessing, ended in demise. His downfall was not immediate; it was a slow drift. Like a fool on a floatie in the middle of the ocean, he let the tide of spiritual ambivalence carry him away from God.

Solomon's tale opens our eyes to the danger of drifting. If the wisest man in the world drifted away from God, how much more susceptible are we? How exactly did this man, known as a mighty man of God, let himself turn away? I'd venture to say he simply got too comfortable and then gradually lost the depth of his relationship with the Lord. It's also possible that his appearance and reputation of godliness inclined him to underestimate the impact of small acts of disobedience and how they would damage his spiritual walk.

Just as Solomon fell away, we may find ourselves resting on rafts of idolatry, self-righteousness, or complacency, slowly drifting from the firm foundation we once had in Christ. We may prioritize others' opinions over God's truth, believe we know it all, or mistake indifference toward God for comfort with God.

It's often the distractions in our lives that lead to a drift. It creeps up like a gentle snooze, lulling us into a spiritual slumber, until one day we open our eyes and realize how much we've gone astray. If that happens, we do not need to remain lost because God is always within reach. We can find our way to the shores of his mercy if we turn back to him.

Instead of succumbing to the drift of distraction, let us pick up the oar of obedience, fix our eyes on God, and strive to remain grounded in Christ. And if we open our eyes one day and realize we've floated away from God, let us remember that he will always draw us close and welcome us back with open arms.

Whenever you begin to lose sight of God's goodness or become so swept up in familiar patterns that you feel the spiritual distance setting in, reach for the mighty hand of Jesus. His grace is a lifeline and stronger than anything that may try to carry you away.

Reflect

- How might you be drifting from God? How will you reach for his hand today?
- How can you continue to cultivate your faith and passion for God?

Lord, help me not to mistake comfort with complacency in my walk. Fill me with more passion and help me to serve you authentically in every area of my life. Keep me from drifting away. In Jesus' name. Amen.

34

Same Old Snake

The serpent was the shrewdest of all the wild animals the LORD God had made. One day he asked the woman, "Did God really say you must not eat the fruit from any of the trees in the garden?"

GENESIS 3:1 NLT

You'd be hard-pressed to find a Christian who hasn't, at some point in their walk, wondered what the heck Adam and Eve were thinking. Many of us have thoughts like "Well, thanks a lot, Eve," "Way to man up, Adam," or "I'm gonna have a lot to say to them when we meet in heaven!"

It's not uncommon for us to read Genesis 3 and wonder how different the world would have been if Adam and Eve had not been so hardheaded—if they never ate the fruit, if humankind had never fallen. But while Adam and Eve do share the responsibility for allowing sin to enter the world, we must not overlook how the crafty serpent tempted them to defy God in the first place.

Adam and Eve lived in the garden of Eden that God had planted. There, the two of them walked in complete peace and unity with God. They had freedom to eat anything except for the fruit from the Tree of Knowledge of Good and Evil. In Genesis 2:16–17, God commanded the man, saying, "You may surely eat of every tree of the garden, but of the tree of the knowledge of good and evil you shall not eat, for in the day that you eat of it you shall surely die" (ESV).

Yet, when the serpent—the devil—spoke to Eve, he cunningly twisted God's command, planting seeds of doubt and desire in her mind. He used a threefold strategy to tempt Eve, appealing to what the Bible later describes as "the lust of the flesh, the lust of the eyes, and the pride of life" (1 John 2:16 NIV).

First, the devil appealed to the lust of the flesh. The lying, sneaky serpent enticed Eve by making the forbidden fruit appear good. Genesis 3:6 tells us that Eve "saw that the fruit of the tree was good for food" (NIV). Interestingly enough, this is the first time in the Bible that anyone other than God saw something as good. In creation, God repeatedly "saw that it was good," but when Eve saw good, it hinted at how the Enemy had subtly convinced Eve to trust her own judgment instead of God's.

The devil's second attempt was to tempt Eve with the lust of the eyes. The serpent directed Eve's focus to the fruit's appearance, which was "pleasing to the eye." After seeing that the fruit was pleasing, Eve began to value her perception over God's clear command, suggesting she could determine what was beautiful and desirable independently of God's word.

Third, the devil tempted Eve through the pride of life. The serpent promised Eve that eating the fruit would make her "like God, knowing good and evil" (v. 5 NIV). This temptation filled her with a desire for power. She believed the lie that she could discern good and evil just as God does.

Notice the progression: Eve saw that the fruit was good, saw that it was pleasing to the eye, and saw that it was useful for gaining wisdom. In each instance, she trusted her own judgment over God's, a trust that led her and humankind to fall into sin. And here's the thing: while we are no longer in Eden, the serpent is still tempting us to trust our discernment over God's.

Just as Eve continuously saw that sin seemed "good," we, too, are susceptible to making the same mistake. We may think we know what's best when things appear good and feel right. But our own understanding can quickly lead us astray. That's why we must be vigilant to walk by faith, not sight. Our perception paves the way for deception, but God's instruction provides divine protection.

We need to remember that what may seem good in our eyes isn't always good in God's eyes. Instead of leaning on our own perceptions, we must trust God's wisdom. His instructions are our protection, guiding us toward what is truly good. Let's choose to live in accordance with God's will and not fall for the same old tricks from the same old snake.

Reflect

- In what areas of your life do you find yourself trusting your own judgment more than God's guidance?
- How can you guard yourself from "the lust of the flesh, the lust of the eyes, and the pride of life" (1 John 2:16 NIV)?

Jesus, thank you for saving us from sin and giving us the discernment to recognize the plans of the Enemy. Help me to be discerning and not to fall for the devil's schemes. Thank you for your protection and grace. In Jesus' name. Amen.

35

Beyond Bethesda

When Jesus saw him lying there and knew that he had already been there a long time, he said to him, "Do you want to be healed?"

JOHN 5:6 ESV

Day by day, the sick would come to the pool of Bethesda. It was a pool with waters known to bring healing and hope, restoring the lives of the afflicted. People came and went, receiving their healing, but a sick man had been there for thirty-eight years, watching people step into the waters and emerge healed, their ailments washed away by the so-called miracle waters.

With a mixture of hope and resignation, the man waited for his opportunity to be made well, convinced that if he could just make it to the water, everything would change. Day after day, year after year, the man clung to the belief that this pool was his only chance for healing. But he needed someone to help him get to the waters because he couldn't make it on his own. For decades no one came. That is, no one until Jesus.

While the man lay watching as he always did, Jesus approached him and asked, "Do you want to be healed?" Likely taken aback by the question, the man replied, saying, "I have no one to help me into the pool when the water is stirred. While I am trying to get in, someone else goes down ahead of me" (John 5:7 NIV).

Jesus was unfazed by the man's obstacles, and with a power much greater than Bethesda, Jesus issued a clear command: "Get up, pick up your pallet and walk" (v. 8 NASB). No waiting for the water to stir, no need for someone else to assist—just a clear call to action. Immediately, the man was well.

What are the "Bethesdas" in our lives? The places we think we *need* to go, the people we think we *need* to be with, the possessions we think we *need* to have. Like the man at the pool, we often believe that reaching a specific goal or obtaining something we desire will make us whole, that everything would change if we could just achieve that one thing.

Perhaps we believe it's the dream that, if attained, will restore our self-worth. Maybe it's the romantic relationship that, if acquired, will rid us of loneliness. Perhaps it's the home that, if purchased, will provide us a sense of security. Maybe it's the career achievement that, if reached, will finally make us feel valued.

Sometimes, without realizing it, we try to heal our inner wounds by changing our external realities. We try our best to reach the currents of change, but we somehow continue to find ourselves lying on the sidelines, watching others receive all that we long for. While we may cling to the hope that something or someone will finally cure the ache in our hearts, we may eventually grow discouraged.

As Proverbs 13:12 says, "Hope deferred makes the heart sick, but when the desire comes, it is a tree of life" (NKJV). The cure to our afflictions is not found in our "Bethesdas;" our true remedy is only found in Jesus. The man at Bethesda believed his healing first depended on reaching the waters, but Jesus showed him that his healing wasn't about the pool—it was about trusting Jesus' command.

Jesus invites us to look beyond temporary fixes and see him as the true source of healing and fulfillment. When Jesus asked, "Do you want to be healed?" he was challenging the man to look beyond the pool to an entirely new possibility—one that didn't depend on circumstances but on faith in Jesus. "Get up, pick up your mat, and walk" was a call to action, a step away from passivity toward faith.

Jesus asks us the same question today: "Do you want to be healed?" He calls us to stop waiting for perfect conditions and to trust him instead. Our healing and wholeness aren't found in reaching a particular milestone but in stepping out in faith toward Christ, who meets all our needs.

Are there areas where you've been waiting for change, believing some earthly thing will finally make you feel whole? Look beyond your "Bethesdas" and trust in Jesus. It's time to pick up your mat and walk, leaving behind the waiting and simply trusting in the one who truly heals.

Reflect

- How can you focus more on seeking Jesus for your fulfillment rather than specific outcomes?
- What step of faith is Jesus calling you to take today?

Lord, please reveal areas in my life where I may be looking to Bethesda instead of you. Help me not to seek fulfillment in people, places, or things; help me instead to put all my hope in you. Thank you for making me well. In Jesus' name. Amen.

36

The Weight of Fruitfulness

He is like a tree planted beside flowing streams that bears its fruit in its season, and its leaf does not wither. Whatever he does prospers.

Psalm 1:3 CSB

As a child, I loved going to the grocery store with my mom and weighing fruit on the produce scale. The more fruit I added, the heavier it got, and as my mother explained, more weight comes at a higher cost. This simple childhood memory reminds me of the spiritual journey we undertake as followers of Christ, particularly when it comes to the fruits of the Holy Spirit.

At first glance, we often think of the fruits of the Spirit as positive attributes that enhance our lives and bring us closer to God, and they certainly do. But, like fruit on a scale, a certain weight comes with carrying these qualities in abundance. The more fruit God produces in us—love, joy, peace, patience, kindness, goodness, faithfulness, gentleness, and self-control

(Galatians 5:22–23)—the more we feel the weight of that fruit in our lives.

When God produces more fruit in us, it often means he is preparing us to carry a heavier load, to stretch beyond our comfort zones, and to trust him more deeply. The cost of carrying this fruit is often a refining process—a pruning as Jesus describes it in John 15:2, where he says, "Every branch that does bear fruit he prunes, that it may bear more fruit" (ESV).

Pruning can be a painful but necessary process for us. Maybe the fruit of love calls us to forgive someone who hurt us deeply, even though it feels impossible. The fruit of joy might urge us to express gratitude in the midst of suffering. The fruit of peace might require us to trust God fully when everything around us is uncertain. The fruit of patience might force us to wait. And the fruits of kindness, gentleness, and self-control might order us to practice restraint in what we say and be mindful of what we do.

All of these fruits produce good things in our lives, but the weight of carrying them can feel heavy, especially when we are faced with ongoing challenges that test our character and resolve. Think about tree branches that bend from the weight of the fruit they bear. This is not a sign of weakness but abundance.

God uses the weight of spiritual fruit to strengthen us. However, this growth and pruning process requires grit and a willingness to be pruned by

God. It comes with difficulty, discomfort, and strain. We may mistake the heaviness as a problem, but in reality, it is simply the holy pressure of God's hand upon us, blessing and pruning areas in our hearts. Gently removing habits, mindsets, relationships, or character traits that hinder our growth in him.

Being fruitful in the Spirit isn't always easy, but it is always worth it. The apostle Paul reminds us in 2 Corinthians 4:17, "For our light and momentary troubles are achieving for us an eternal glory that far outweighs them all" (NIV). The weight we feel from bearing spiritual fruit is merely momentary when compared to the eternal rewards of living a life that reflects God's character.

When we feel the burden of the fruit we carry, we can take comfort in knowing that God is with us, providing the strength we need to continue growing and producing even more fruit. Let us not shy away from the challenges that come with this growth but embrace them, remembering that they are shaping us into who God has called us to be.

Each step we take, each moment of pruning we endure, and each piece of fruit we bear is a testament to God's transformative power in our lives. As we press on, we do so with the confidence that the weight of fruitfulness is not a burden but a blessing—proof that God is nurturing our growth and producing fruit that will last.

Reflect

- Reflect on a time when you felt the weight of spiritual growth. What did God teach you through that experience?
- What practical steps can you take to cultivate the fruits of the Spirit more intentionally in your daily life?

Jesus, thank you for the fruits of the Holy Spirit. May I be like a firm tree: rooted deeply in you and bearing much fruit for your glory. In Jesus' name. Amen.

37

On One A-Chord

Just as the body is one and has many members, and all the members of the body, though many, are one body, so it is with Christ.

1 CORINTHIANS 12:12 ESV

There's something beautiful about a choir. All the different voices blend together to create a harmonious sound. The bass singers provide a strong foundation, the altos and tenors add rich harmony, and the sopranos carry the melody.

But imagine a bass trying to unleash an inner Mariah Carey or a soprano suddenly belting out a solo in a Barry White register. You'd have voices cracking like eggs on a Sunday morning, turning harmony into full-blown cacophony. The beauty of the choir would not have been lost because of a lack of talent; it would become lost because members stepped out of their roles. Each voice is unique, so when someone abandons their part, the entire performance suffers.

Just as a choir requires each member to stay true to their voice, the body of Christ thrives when each person embraces their God-given qualities. God has given each of us different gifts, roles, and talents. As Paul writes in Romans 12:4–5,

> For as we have many members in one body, but all the members do not have the same function, so we, being many, are one body in Christ, and individually members of one another. (NKJV)

Paul's message to the early church (and to us today) is clear: unity in Christ does not mean uniformity. We are not called to think the same, act the same, or possess the same gifts. In fact, our diversity is intentional and God-given. Every gift is vital to the body of Christ, whether it's teaching, serving, encouraging, giving, or leading. The church becomes a beautiful symphony, working in harmony for the glory of God.

And yes, maintaining this harmony requires intentional effort and willingness to embrace the roles God has given us and others. This means we must be vigilant to correct ourselves if we begin to fall into the mindset of comparison.

Comparison opens the door to insecurity and arrogance. These two qualities may seem to fall on opposite ends of the spectrum—insecurity being an underestimation of worth and arrogance an overestimation of it, but they are both rooted in pride and self-centeredness. And the Enemy uses both to promote division and distract us from Christ.

Whether through feelings of inadequacy or an inflated sense of self-importance, comparison interferes with the greater purpose for which we were created. Scripture reminds us,

> Do nothing out of selfish ambition or vain conceit. Rather, in humility value others above yourselves, not looking to your own interests but each of you to the interests of the others. (Philippians 2:3–4 NIV)

Insecurity may lead us to question our place in the body or withhold our gifts, while arrogance convinces us that our way is the only way, the best way, creating an atmosphere where others feel undervalued, unrespected, or excluded. And that is not what God intends.

However, when we are willing to live a life that is Christ-centered instead of self-centered, we become empowered to see ourselves and others through the eyes of God. Rather than fostering division, we celebrate our collective differences. This level of harmony requires humility, understanding, and mutual respect.

Just as a choir must practice, listen, and follow the conductor's lead, the body of Christ must work together with a shared sense of purpose, following the teachings of Jesus. May we always strive to appreciate the unique gifts that each of us brings, recognizing that we are stronger and more complete when we stand together in our diversity.

By letting go of comparison and embracing the roles God has given us, we build a community that is fully attuned with the melody of God's love. Then we can move on in one accord.

Reflect

- What unique gifts or roles do you believe God has given you within the body of Christ?
- Consider how comparison has affected your sense of purpose or worth. What steps can you take to focus more on Christ and less on comparison?

Abba, whenever I am tempted to compare myself to others, help me look to you instead. Help me find security in your word and humility in the truth that I am radically loved by you. Help me embrace the role you have given me and encourage other believers to do the same. May your body be beautifully different and united. In Jesus' name. Amen.

38

Reign in the Storm

The disciples went and woke him up, shouting, "Lord, save us! We're going to drown!"

MATTHEW 8:25 NLT

If you have been a Christian for any length of time, you've likely heard the story about Jesus taking a nap on a boat in the middle of a storm. Not just in any storm either—we're talking about violent waves, gusting winds, and a boat full of disciples who were afraid they were going to die.

As the sea tossed the boat back and forth, Jesus slept on a cushion in the stern of the boat. In a panic, the disciples rushed to wake him, shouting, "Teacher, don't you care that we're going to drown?" (Mark 4:38). In response, Jesus woke up and spoke to the wind and waves. Immediately, the wind stopped blowing, and the waves stood still. Jesus then said to his disciples, "Why are you afraid? Do you still have no faith?" (v. 40).

Jesus had just done something unthinkable; the disciples were absolutely terrified because. What kind of man could command the wind and the sea to obey him? For the sake of empathizing, let's pretend for a moment that we were in this exact situation.

I am guessing that, like the disciples, the intensity of the storm would leave most of us in horror. As water lapped into the boat, we, too, would frantically wake Jesus from his peaceful nap. Then, when Jesus woke up, he would ask us why we were afraid. Many of us would probably say—or at the very least think—*Jesus, with all due respect, what do you mean by 'Why am I afraid?' Do you not see the tremendous tempest attempting to take my life?*

While there was clearly a valid reason for the disciples to be afraid, I wonder if Jesus was not inquiring about their natural fear of the waves but more so about their lack of faith in him. After all they had witnessed him do, did the disciples not believe Jesus was powerful enough to act on their behalf, even when it looked as if he was doing nothing?

Maybe the disciples hadn't realized the extent of Jesus' power or maybe their panic prevented them from thinking things through. Either way, when Jesus woke and spoke to the storm, the wind and sea obeyed him. There was no more room for confusion. Silencing the storm was not simply a demonstration of power; it was a revelation of Jesus' divinity.

Still, we may ask ourselves, "Why was Jesus sleeping in the first place?" The answer (at least on this side of heaven) is that we don't know. Maybe he was soothed to sleep by the sound of rain. Maybe he hardly slept the night before. No matter the reason, Jesus was able to do something the disciples and many of us struggle to do: be still in the storm.

Jesus did not allow external circumstances to disrupt his internal peace. His ability to rest through a storm wasn't a sign of disregard for the disciples; it was a sign of regard for his father. Jesus knew who he was and what his Father could do, which made it possible for him to tap into a supernatural calm in the midst of chaos.

Because of Christ's work on the cross, we, too, can access supernatural peace. However, when life's storms crash against the deck of our souls, we may struggle to hold onto that peace if our hearts and minds are too consumed by fear. A swirl of emotions and thoughts can make it difficult to see beyond the current storm—be it financial strain, relationship struggles, health issues, or deep emotional pain.

In those moments, we may look to Jesus and call out to him for help but also wonder if our cry is falling on God's sleeping ears. We may look at our lives and feel the biting winds of worry pushing us to doubt. But, when it appears that God has left us to drown in the difficulties we're facing, we must know that he is indeed working, even if we don't see it.

God's silence is not a sign of abandonment; it is a call to deeper dependence. It is an opportunity for us to learn to rest in who he is—no matter the intensity of the storm. Through prayer, connection with community, and meditation on God's sovereignty, we can find the strength to face every storm.

Even in our darkest moments, when God feels silent, we must remember this promise: God will never leave us nor forsake us (Deuteronomy 31:8). This assurance is not based on our feelings or circumstances but on the unchanging nature of God himself.

We may not always understand why God allows us to go through certain trials or why he chooses to remain quiet at times, but we can trust that no matter how heavy the rain, we serve a God who reigns—a God who can speak peace to every storm.

Reflect

- When have you felt God was silent in your life, and how did you respond?
- How can you learn to trust God's presence more deeply?

Lord, I will trust you in every trial and remember that you are able to silence the storm. Help me to have expectant faith and not to be overcome by the winds of worry or waves of despair. May I learn to rest in your peace no matter how chaotic my circumstances become. In Jesus' name. Amen.

39

Kindness Isn't Niceness

[Jesus] went into the temple and began to throw out those who were selling, and he said, "It is written, 'My house will be a house of prayer,' but you have made it a den of thieves!"

LUKE 19:45–46 CSB

There is a common trope in movies where parents go out of town for the weekend and their impressionable teen gets peer-pressured into throwing a *small* get-together at their house—without their parents' knowledge. While the initial idea of a party is met with apprehension, eventually the teen agrees to have a few people over, "so long as things don't get out of hand."

Well, things most certainly always go too far. Before they know it, their parents' house is packed with strangers engaging in reckless behavior, and the mob of people grows completely out of control. Then, just when it seems that things couldn't get any worse, the parents walk through the door in complete horror and disbelief.

Though this is a common occurrence in movies, we also see a similar example of this in the Bible. In Matthew 21:12–17, we find an interesting story involving Jesus, disobedient children, and a whole lot of tables. Imagine this: Jesus walks into the temple—a sacred house of prayer where God's presence should be honored and the hearts of the faithful should be uplifted.

But, instead of seeing people honoring God in peace and reverence, Jesus finds the temple full of people fighting and yelling. Birds flying around all over the place, merchants selling goods, and people buying them. This was not only unexpected—it was detestable. To say Jesus was upset would be an understatement. He was overcome with righteous anger.

In a manner that some might find a bit harsh, Jesus confronted the situation directly by flipping over the tables of the money changers, kicking the chairs of the dove merchants, and demanding that everyone who set up shop get out. He said to them, "It is written: 'My House Will Be Called A House Of Prayer'; but you are making it a Den Of Robbers" (v. 13 NASB).

At first glance, Jesus' behavior might seem out of character, but it was not. This was not just a case of someone losing their temper; this was God standing firm for righteousness. While the actions Jesus took may not be "nice," they were incredibly kind. Because while niceness and kindness are often confused, they are not the same thing.

Niceness is about being agreeable, pleasant, and avoiding conflict; it's about saying what people want to hear or keeping the peace to make others feel comfortable. Kindness, on the other hand, is about seeking the highest good of others, even when it requires speaking hard truths or taking actions that might seem harsh on the surface. Kindness is rooted in love and a desire for righteousness.

In the temple, Jesus wasn't concerned with being "nice" to the merchants and money changers. Instead, Jesus displayed kindness by cleansing the temple and removing the barriers that kept people from experiencing a genuine relationship with God.

As followers of Christ, we are called to be kind, but that doesn't always sound or look very nice. This does not mean we should intentionally disregard others' feelings or fail to consider their needs, but it does imply that we should never let others' comfort take precedence over God's commands.

Ephesians 4:15 encourages us to "[speak] the *truth* in *love*" (CSB, emphasis added). The balance between truth and love is crucial for believers: we are to uphold truth while being motivated by love. This means finding the courage to speak up and act according to God's Word—even when it's easier to stay silent or follow the crowd. It may mean encouraging a friend to make better choices or standing firm in our faith when others waver. Kindness may occasionally require us to flip a few tables, but it upholds accountability, honesty, integrity, and courage.

In the end, kindness is about more than making people feel good; it's about helping them grow closer to God and protecting what is holy. So, when faced with a choice between being nice or being kind, choose kindness. It's not always the easiest path, but it's the most loving. After all, Jesus didn't come to keep everyone comfortable; he came to transform lives. And sometimes, that transformation requires us to flip a few tables ourselves.

Reflect

- Are there habits, relationships, or situations that distract you from fully living out your faith? How can you "flip these tables" in your life?
- Do you prioritize kindness or niceness? How can you show more kindness in your daily life?

Lord, thank you for your loving kindness and correction. Fill me with courage and help me to become more kind. In Jesus' name. Amen.

40

He Bore it All

"He himself bore our sins" in his body on the cross, so that we might die to sins and live for righteousness; "by his wounds you have been healed."

1 Peter 2:24 NIV

A few years ago, I worked in a group home for teenage survivors of child trafficking. It was the most challenging but Christ-centered work I have ever done. By nature, this job involved working with teens who had experienced unimaginable trauma, and while I initially understood the work would be difficult, I failed to understand how much this work would teach me about the love of God.

One night, a young girl who struggled with self-harm began to experience a moment of crisis. Relying on the guidance of the Lord and all of the training we had received, I began to implement crisis intervention techniques. In the midst of doing all that I could to prevent her from harming herself, she did something I did not see coming: she harmed me instead.

With all the might that a slim thirteen-year-old girl could muster, she punched me in the arm and then spat in my face. Suddenly, a rush of silent rage replaced my gentleness and resolve. My pride was pricked, and my ego was bruised. How could someone I had been nothing but kind to treat me in such a way? Unable to speak from the shock of it all, I watched the young girl storm away with no remorse or apology.

I remember sitting on a stoop and staring up at the night sky, crying out to God for help. I was livid. Appalled by this child's behavior, I wrestled with the "Oh no she didn't" parts of my heart. I did not deserve to be treated that way, and I made sure to let the Lord know it. I continued to cry out to God about all the wrong I had experienced, and he addressed me in a manner that the Holy Spirit normally does. I heard that still, small voice say, "But you've done the same to me." Woof—talk about a heart check!

After hearing the Holy Spirit's words, my mind suddenly filled with images of the cross, nail-pierced hands, blood, and a crown of thorns upon my Savior's head. The Spirit reminded me that my Jesus was spat on, belittled, and beaten beyond recognition. He bore all of that not for any wrong he had done but for every wrong I had done. In that moment, I realized that the pain I felt wasn't even a sliver of the pain Jesus endured for me—and the pain he endured for you.

Even when we were lost in sin, rebelling against him and rejecting his love, Jesus chose to bear it all. He bore our sins, our failures, our mistakes, and our outright defiance. And he did it willingly, out of pure love and grace. So, when we are called to love like Jesus, we might get a little hurt in the process. We might be called to minister to people who do not want to receive what we have to offer. We might just have to pick up our cross (Luke 9:23).

As it is written in Matthew 5:44, "I say to you, love your enemies, bless those who curse you, do good to those who hate you, and pray for those who spitefully use you and persecute you" (NKJV). At first glance, this verse may seem like an affront to our honor, but we must remember that loving our enemies is exactly what Jesus has done for us.

Jesus hung upon the cross and said, "Father, forgive them, for they don't know what they are doing" (Luke 23:34 NLT). He died upon the cross but rose again so that, through him, we could have the gift of eternal life. He spared us from the punishment we deserve, and he adorned us with blessings we don't deserve.

Many months later, after this young girl was accepted into a foster home, I was told she expressed remorse for what she had done in her anger. Like this young girl, I realized that all of us are in need of a home, of love, of forgiveness. All of us are in need of Jesus. So when you find yourself being challenged in love, remember that Jesus is the only one who perfectly expressed it. Remember the one who bore it all.

Reflect

- When you feel wronged or hurt, how can you remember Jesus' sacrifice and choose to respond with grace and forgiveness?
- What areas of your life need more of Jesus' example of unconditional love and sacrifice?

Jesus, thank you for forgiving me of my sins and for bearing it all. I put my faith in you and will choose to love even when it's difficult. In Jesus' name. Amen.

Acknowledgments

This book is the fulfillment of a prayer I said many years ago and a reminder that God's promises are yes and amen (2 Corinthians 1:20). God used this experience to reveal so much to me about who he is and what I needed to surrender in my heart.

I would like to thank my family and my loved ones who supported me through the process of writing this book. I am incredibly thankful for each person who has lifted me up in prayer—known and unknown—and each person who purchases this book. It has been an incredible honor and privilege to write it.

I would like to thank everyone at BroadStreet Publishing for believing in me and coming alongside me in this writing process.

Thank you to every single follower, subscriber, and person whose support helped me accomplish this dream.

Most of all, I would like to give my greatest thanks and appreciation for God, who carried me through many storms, taught me profound lessons, and used his beautiful words to show me just how much he loves humankind.

If it had not been for Jesus and all he has done for me, I would not be here to testify of his goodness but for God. He is a loving Father, incredible friend, and mighty Savior. He is the source of my strength and the one who gave me the courage to write.

To God and everyone else, I am eternally grateful.

About the Author

Hillary Phillips is an actress, voice-over artist, and content creator. *My Brain While Reading the Bible* is her debut devotional combining her faith, humor, and heart and written to uplift and encourage others.

Whether through writing or performing, Hillary strives to bring joy and foster spiritual growth in the lives of others. When she's not behind a computer or a camera, she loves reporting for auntie duty, reading a good book, laughing with her loved ones, and staying active.

In everything she does, Hillary strives to please God and shine his light.